IQBAL AHMED was born in Kashmir in 1968 and has lived in London since 1994. *Sorrows of the Moon* is his first book and was chosen as Book of the Year in the *Guardian* and the *Independent on Sunday*. His second book, *Empire of the Mind*, is also available from Constable and Robinson Ltd. He is currently working on a novel.

Praise for *Sorrows of the Moon*

'Iqbal Ahmed loves people, cities, details, history and poetry with a true, clear, writterly attention. The structures and appalling current dilemma of his own birthplace were created by the empire run from this city – this London seen by the sad, learned, compassionate eyes of a man from Srinagar. Read it and weep and be grateful for its subtlety, courtesy and depth.'

Ruth Padel, Chair, The Poetry Society

'Like Baudelaire's sorrowful moon he "drops a furtive tear" for his homeland; but perhaps we are left with a sliver of hope in the image of Ahmed's old moon and his new united in a single vision.'

Sameer Rahim, *TLS*

Also by Iqbal Ahmed

Empire of the Mind

Sorrows of the Moon

In Search of London

IQBAL AHMED

CONSTABLE • LONDON

Constable & Robinson Ltd
3 The Lanchesters
162 Fulham Palace Road
London W6 9ER
www.constablerobinson.com

First published in the UK in 2004 by Coldstream Publishers,
27 Savernake Road, London NW3 2JT

This edition published by Constable,
an imprint of Constable & Robinson Ltd 2007

Designed and produced in Great Britain by Clinton Smith Design

A copy of the British Library Cataloguing in
Publication Data is available from the British Library.

ISBN: 978-1-84529-517-2

Printed and bound in the EU

1 3 5 7 9 10 8 6 4 2

Quand parfois sur ce globe, en sa langueur oisive,
Elle laisse filer une larme furtive,
Un poëte pieux, ennemi du sommeil…

When sometimes from her stupefying calm
On to this earth she drops a furtive tear
Pale as an opal, iridescent, rare…

Baudelaire: 'Sorrows of the Moon', *Les Fleurs du Mal*

Contents

1	A Borough Called Tower Hamlets	9
2	Soul of a Soulless City: The City	25
3	Abuja to London	46
4	A Kiosk in Charing Cross Road	61
5	Post Office Counters Limited	79
6	London Taxis International	97
7	Mariam in Marylebone	119
8	Bloomsbury Blues	140
9	Across Waterloo Bridge	160
10	The False Reputation of Hampstead	176

A Borough
Called Tower Hamlets

For several years, I shunned the borough of Tower Hamlets in East London. Its name evoked a claustrophobic vision of tower blocks in my subconscious mind, rather than a picture of hamlets around the Tower of London. It was distressing for me to set out on an excursion into this neighbourhood. Then one day, a London taxi-driver confided in me, having read his daily paper, that there were 50,000 Talibans living in Tower Hamlets. He had confused the elderly Bengali men, who wore white beards and skullcaps, with the Afghan fighters. Among all the races in India, the East India Company men had found only two races who were less martial – the men of Bengal and those of Kashmir. Therefore, I had a kinship with the people living in Tower Hamlets whom I had avoided while residing in London.

On a Saturday morning, I cut through the City, which was built in the nineteenth century on the wealth generated by foreign trade with the colonies, to reach Commercial Road. I passed the Royal Exchange and a building made of convoluted iron, which I knew existed though I was uncertain about its location. When I reached Aldgate, I asked someone for directions to Brick Lane. The man thought that I was heading for Sonali Bank in Brick Lane. I was meeting Anwar Mian that morning to see his workshop, and he would guide me through his neighbourhood. I turned into a side-street from Commercial Road, which becomes Brick Lane after an intersection. The images of the architecture of the city had persisted in my eyes, and I was blinded for a few moments to witness the clutter of Brick Lane. I wondered about the people who stayed at a nondescript building called City Hotel: bankers visiting the City, or people visiting their relatives in Brick Lane? No, it was too cheap for the former and too dear for the latter. The hotel overlooked a derelict yard and there was a monumental mason nearby, displaying tombstones in marble and granite. Brick Lane was dug up for roadworks, and the whole street was roped off except for the pavements.

There was a crowd outside what looked like a betting-shop. But it turned out to be a facility for sending money abroad, displaying exchange rates on bulletin boards. On the other side of the road, a dingy-looking shop sold haberdashery. There were also a few shops along this road selling synthetic fabrics. A radio blasted Hindi film songs from a record shop. A prevailing smell of curry emanated from the numerous restaurants on both sides of the street. The restaurants looked narrow with two rows of tables fitted in, but most of them were well-kept. These were the restaurants that had made Brick Lane well-known. A pile of empty tins of purified butter and cooking oils was lying on the pavement, to be collected by binmen. The pavement felt greasy around the lampposts. Brick Lane was getting ready for its annual curry festival: there were banners and posters everywhere announcing its date.

Anwar Mian used the upper floor of a shed as his workshop, which was located at the rear of the houses in Fashion Street. I climbed up a makeshift staircase to reach its entrance. Anwar opened the door for me and ushered me into his workshop. There were four elderly machinists stitching leather jackets, and Anwar himself had been skilfully cutting patterns on a wooden bench. I would have liked to let Anwar carry on with his work while finding out from him what it was like to live in Tower Hamlets. But his workshop was full of tailoring accessories and there was nowhere I could take a seat. He carried out all the stages of making a leather garment in a small room. Anwar took off the apron he wore to show me around Brick Lane.

I searched in vain for a coffee shop. In the end, I decided to sit down with Anwar in a take-away-style restaurant. The man behind the counter mistakenly spoke to me in Bengali while serving us. The food was inexpensive but the regular customers asked for a discount. Anwar had started his workshop five years ago after going bankrupt in the restaurant business. He said that it was wrong to assume that Indian restaurants in London never went bust. He owed a large sum of money to a bank, and it was impossible for him to go into the restaurant business again. Therefore, he had borrowed a small amount from his elder sister whose husband was a businessman. He had bought his second-hand machines from a Brick Lane resident who couldn't make it in the leather trade. Having declared himself bankrupt in the previous business, Anwar could get no financial assistance from anywhere. He found a shed nearby to put the machines in. Anwar considered himself fortunate to have employed the elderly men as machinists, because they showed patience whenever he couldn't pay them on time. Also, he didn't have to pay for the raw material. It was supplied by the retailers for whom he made the leather garments. The retailers paid him £23 to make a jacket. The wholesalers in Brick lane sold the leather jackets for less than £20 each. But the retailers preferred to have their own label on the jackets: 'Made in Great Britain'.

Anwar agreed to take me around the corner to a wholesaler in the area to view his shop. The owner of the business had gone to Jamme Masjid for the midday prayer. Anwar decided to show me the nearby mosque where the wholesaler had gone to pray. The words 'Jamme Masjid' were written in bad handwriting in Arabic. Even in poor countries the Jamme Masjids are adorned with calligraphic writing. On the other side of the building, the sundial had '1743-Umbra Sumus' engraved on it.

The shop had opened when we returned after a few

minutes. It was the same size as Anwar's workshop, but it was packed to the ceiling with leather garments. It also had a basement, which was accessible through a small trapdoor. While we were standing in the shop a stout man emerged from the basement, bringing the stock out and loading it into a private cab bound for a retailer in the West End. A couple of fashion students were choosing lambskin remnants in one corner of the shop. It seemed that they didn't have enough cash to pay for the small bundle, but the wholesaler accepted a cheque from them for £20.

On leaving the shop, we walked towards the north end of Brick Lane. The chimney of the old Truman Brewery, which had been given a new glass front, stood tall between the two ends of the road. Men in suits carrying portfolios were going in and out of the building. I was curious about their occupation. Anwar explained that the old brewery had been turned into a centre for fashion and information technology, and also that there was an artesian well beneath it. Across the road, I saw the art gallery, which had been brought to life a year ago by a certain professor through an exhibition of cadavers. As we passed the brewery, Brick Lane changed its character. The restaurants gave way to clothing shops run by artists and designers who specialized in street fashion. They sold combat trousers, hipster skirts and kimono tops in outrageous colours. The leather shops appeared again towards the end of the road. The black mannequins in the show-windows of the leather shops had collected a thick layer of dust. Notices affixed to their doors read 'Open to the Public'. But these small shops were actually operated by big wholesalers. The wholesaler whose shop I had been to with Anwar had one more shop along the same road.

Anwar lived in the neighbourhood, in a block of flats owned by the council. He invited me to his home for tea. We took a lift to the fifth floor of a big building. Some bags of rubbish had been left outside the flats, ready for disposal, and I saw a chute cupboard for the disposal of rubbish near the lift. Anwar lived in a two-bedroom flat, together with his mother, wife and two younger sisters. He and his wife occupied one bedroom, and his mother and two sisters slept in the other. I wondered about the children I had seen playing outside the flat. Anwar said they were his nephews and nieces, who had come to see them. His elder brother and sister had moved out of the flat a few years ago. Anwar was twenty-eight years old. His father had died when he was fourteen. His family had moved to the East End from Sylhet in Bangladesh twenty years ago. Anwar's father had lived and worked in Whitechapel for ten years before bringing his wife and children over. Anwar said that he was very fond of his father, who had died of a heart attack at the age of forty-eight. It became his responsibility to look after the family when his brother moved out.

Anwar's wife brought tea and biscuits for us. She was shy and demure, and spoke very little English. Anwar had been to Sylhet a year ago and stayed there for six months to find a suitable girl to marry. He had a very big wedding in Sylhet. His family had invited over a thousand guests, and it had cost him £2,000 to feed them. He spoke with modest pride about his wedding. I asked him why he decided to go to Sylhet to find a wife when there was no dearth of Bengali girls in Whitechapel. He said that it was difficult for him to relate to a Bengali girl born in Whitechapel, even though both of his younger sisters were born in the flat where he lived. I could sense the difference between his wife and his sisters, who had a certain East End brashness about them. By marrying a girl from Sylhet, Anwar had made the gulf between himself and the world outside Whitechapel wider. He said that it was the wish of all the elderly Bengali men living in Tower Hamlets to be buried in Sylhet when they die, not in Whitechapel, so their corpses were returned to the soil that had been tilled by their forefathers.

The problems of Anwar's family were the same as those of the Borough of Tower Hamlets. It was the poorest in London, and it had the highest population density in inner London. It also had a high percentage of children who belonged to Bengali families. I left Anwar's flat in a pensive mood. A group of women chatted at the street corner, chewing betel leaves with parings of areca nut, oblivious of the traffic moving in that direction. One of them was carrying jackfruit in her lap. I entered the Whitechapel Gallery for distraction, but I couldn't concentrate on the pictures there. It was the proximity of the City and its grand architecture to a slum which I found disconcerting. I wanted to take a detour, so that the City didn't falsify my sense of reality again.

After a gap of a few months, I returned to Brick Lane to meet Anwar again. The roadwork hadn't been finished and a part of the road was being resurfaced. There were builders working on many properties along this road. The clothing shops displayed gear for the builders in their windows. A closed-down shop appeared after every few shops, complementing the rundown look of the flats above them. The area was a continuous building site. I remembered what Anwar had told me last time: that Brick Lane was not a place for tourists. In fact, I saw a small group of Americans set out on a walking tour to witness the poverty in the area. The guide was explaining the meaning of the word 'ghetto' to them. He said that it was an Italian word, meaning foundry, and had been applied to the site of the first such place in Venice during Medieval times. The tourists stood outside 19 Princelet Street, which their guide told them was 'a museum of diversity'. Some of the Americans wanted to see it but the museum was rarely open to the public. Even though it was the only one of its kind in Britain, if not in Europe, the trustees needed funding to keep the doors of this museum open permanently. I learnt later that this place was exploring how London has always been shaped by new people from different countries and the museum was founded by the people whose ancestors had come to London as refugees.

It was here in Brick Lane that the distressing word 'refugee' had entered the English vocabulary, when French Protestants settled here after fleeing Catholic France towards the end of the seventeenth century. The Huguenots brought the silk weaving industry with them. The second wave of immigrants were Ashkenazi Jews, fleeing from Eastern and Central Europe during the 1880s to escape persecution. Many of them had arrived in London destitute, and found shelter around Brick Lane. They found work in tailoring workshops, which is why tailoring was considered by many people in London to be a Jewish trade. The third wave of immigrants came from Sylhet to escape poverty, only to live an abject life in Tower Hamlets. I was fearful of visiting Whitechapel, because its streets could haunt a nervous traveller like myself.

Looking for Petticoat Lane to browse at its market stalls before meeting Anwar, I was told by someone that it was actually called Middlesex Street. One could not mention the word 'trousers' in front of a lady during Victorian times, and it was considered obscene to mention the word 'petticoat' in front of a gentleman. I had no trouble in saying 'petticoat' when I was young, but I was overcome with shyness to pronounce a place-name which ended in 'sex'. On reaching Petticoat Lane, I was surprised to find out that no trading took place in the market on Saturdays, unlike Portobello Road Market, which traded only on Saturdays. The tradition of the forerunners of the present Petticoat Lane Market, of observing Sabbath on Saturdays, was followed even now.

I was puzzled to see the Metropolitan Police operating from a shop in Brick Lane, instead of a fortified building like those used elsewhere in London. Perhaps it was to give a sense of protection to the Bengali community. I met Anwar in the same place where we had eaten during our last encounter. He was wearing a long collarless shirt embroidered round the neck. I asked him if he felt secure living and working around Brick Lane. He told me that the second generation of Bengalis from Brick Lane were working outside the Whitechapel area, most of them in various supermarkets. When I arrived in London for the first time and took a trip to a supermarket, I found that all the employees were second-generation Bengali men and women. I believed for many months that the supermarket chain belonged to a Bengali businessman. Anwar said that he had seen very little trouble in the area in recent years except for the nail bomb which went off there a few years ago. Bengalis were placid people who kept their heads down. The kingdom of Bengal was conquered by Afghans in the twelfth century (the London taxi-driver believed that Bengalis were the same as Afghans). Anwar said that only Bengali kids got in trouble now and again with the police.

Anwar was busier than before in his workshop, making garments for his customers. He had to deliver his goods to a retailer in the West End that day. I wanted to accompany him on his trip. The cab arrived in the narrow lane where Anwar's workshop was located. The driver, who was from a local cab office, exchanged salaams with Anwar before loading the garments in the boot of his car. His name was Abdul, and he had worked in a restaurant in Brick Lane before becoming a cabbie. He said that he had earned a low wage as a waiter, and people didn't often tip in a Brick Lane restaurant. He had saved £1,000 to buy a car so that he could become self-employed as a taxi-driver. He had joined a local cab firm because he only knew the roads of East London. He could make more money working in the West End as a taxi-driver during the night, but he didn't know how to get in and out of the West End on a Friday night when it is teeming with people. Although it was rough working as a private cab driver in the West End during the weekends, passengers were charged a higher fare than people living in the East End. Abdul's wife had given birth to a baby girl a few days ago. Anwar congratulated him, and asserted his belief that the birth of a child often brings prosperity to a family.

It was a big shop on a main shopping street in the West End. Anwar carried the garments himself to the shop, owned by a Sindhi businessman. There was an overpowering smell of leather inside. The shopkeeper was busy trying to persuade an East European couple to buy a certain jacket. They wanted to know where these garments were made. He picked up a jacket from a pile on Anwar's shoulder and showed them the label with its 'Made in Great Britain' tagline. He was not selling cheap gear from China in his shop, he insisted vigorously. The couple looked convinced by his spiel. He told me later that it takes a lot of persuasion to sell a leather jacket to an East European customer. The shopkeeper said that he started out as a market trader in Petticoat Lane ten years ago, and today he owned several shops in the West End. His experience as a market trader had made him a successful businessman. A tramp who looked stupefied by drink stopped outside the shop. He asked the shopkeeper if he had reached Whitechapel. The shopkeeper was outraged by his remark, and told him that he didn't know where Whitechapel was. Anwar picked up a few bundles of lambskins to take with him to the workshop to make bomber jackets for the retailer. The shopkeeper told Anwar that there was always a good demand for bomber jackets, and he promised to pay him on his next visit.

We travelled by tube from the West End to Brick Lane, Anwar carring a few bundles of nappa leather with him. He told me that it takes patience to survive in the leather trade. It was a seasonal business, and it was the perennial sales in the leather shops that lured a few customers during the summer months. Otherwise, one has to wait six months in a year for the business to pick up. Besides, there are only a few people who are fond of leather garments. Anwar said that it was beyond him to persuade a retail customer to buy a leather jacket. You had to have a certain disposition, like the shopkeeper, to be a salesperson in this trade.

Brick Lane revealed itself in detail on my second visit. I noticed that many chartered accountants had offices above the shops. Perhaps these accountants balanced the books for the owners of the Indian restaurants. Pictures of the Mayor of London as a patron saint of Brick Lane, shaking hands with the restaurant owners, appeared in a number of shop-windows. There were many travel agents in the side-streets, selling tickets for Aeroflot and Biman Airlines. The name 'Katz' was written on a door as a reminder of the past of Brick Lane. When I drifted towards Commercial Street, I discovered a purpose-built soup kitchen for the Jewish poor, erected in 1905. A Baroque church designed by Christopher Wren's apprentice looked outlandish in this setting. A listed building was being converted into lofts as a residence for professional couples. Property prices had already quadrupled around here in the last ten years. The houses in Princelet Street had become quaint. The tailoring workshops of a century before seemed very substantial to me compared to the one occupied by Anwar.

I went back to Anwar's workshop. He wanted to show me the neighbourhood towards Whitechapel. We took a back road from Brick Lane, and when we turned a corner I saw a cash-and-carry hidden behind some small shops in Brick Lane. Bengali women in saris and shawls were buying groceries. The cash-and-carry offered wholesale prices to the general public. Anwar said that there was a huge difference in prices between a supermarket and this cash-and-carry. I thought that a Bengali businessman had done philanthropic work by opening a cash-and-carry here, like a certain banker in Bangladesh who helped the poor.

On reaching Whitechapel Road, Anwar showed me the East London Mosque where he went every Friday for prayers. It had been built in the mid-Eighties with financial aid from an Arab country, since the local population, being mostly poor, could not raise the money. When Peter Gasson revisited *Nairn's London* twenty-two years after the book was first published, he was disconcerted by the sight of a mosque in East London. Whitechapel was made infamous in 1888 by Jack the Ripper, who murdered five women in eight weeks. I used to confuse Whitechapel with Whitehall before I was familiar with the metropolis.

We walked back to Brick Lane along Whitechapel Road. Traffic was heavy, and the pavement was busy with pedestrians. One heard a babel of various languages around here: East London had retained its character. Anwar didn't feel like a victim of racism living in the East End. But he was bothered by pictures published in the tabloids about the changing face of Britain, showing elderly Bengali men wearing white beards and skullcaps, whose only wish was to be buried in the Surma valley of Sylhet, waiting in queues at bus-stops. Anwar didn't remember the time when National Front youths had gone on a rampage in Brick Lane, smashing Bengali shops' windows. He hadn't cast his vote in the general elections. He didn't take part in any national events. He had made peace with himself by living like a pariah in London for the last twenty years. What can be achieved through begging, he said, had ceased to give him pleasure.

It was getting dark and the restaurants in Brick Lane were getting ready for business. A few chefs stood by the restaurant doors waiting for the first diners to walk in. They looked pale, as if the cadavers from the Truman Brewery had come to life. Their faces were discoloured by constant exposure to burning spices in frying pans. Anwar said that the Bengali food is very hot because certain types of green chillies are added to it while cooking. However, the food served in the restaurants in Brick Lane was mild. Even though all the Indian restaurants serve alcohol, he said, many waiters working in those restaurants had never had a sip of alcohol in their life. It was impossible to serve Indian food to English customers without serving them alcohol with it. In fact, these restaurants made their money by selling alcohol, not food, most of them staying open later than eleven at night. Also, English people loved Indian food. Otherwise, how could one find so many restaurants in one street selling the same thing?

Since he had to go back to his workshop to cut some new patterns for his machinists, Anwar bid me farewell and asked me to come and see him again some time. I wanted to cut through the deserted City in the evening. I took Leadenhall Street towards Cheapside, and when I reached the portico of the Lloyd's building, it occurred to me that East India House had once stood here at the corner of Lime Street.

The company's first premises were in the Lord Mayor's great mansion house. It all began here, when the East Indiamen set out on their maiden voyage to India, and Lascars and ayahs crossed the ocean a few centuries later, in the other direction. The Lascars lived in a Home for Asiatics in Limehouse. They were the poorest and most despised group of immigrants living in London. After the opening of the Suez Canal in 1869, European families living in India returned home more regularly. The Memsahibs brought Indian servants with them, who were later abandoned in London. The passports these ayahs carried did not mention the name of their bearers. They had the names of the Memsahibs written on them, like 'Mrs Jones' Ayah'. These servants lived in the Ayahs' Home in Hackney where they kept themselves busy with needlecraft.

Soul of a Soulless City:
The City

During my first few days in London, I stayed at a hostel in Carter Lane, which is located in what cartographers misleadingly refer to as the City. As I stepped out of the hostel, I could see the west façade of St Paul's Cathedral. It was Sunday, and the cathedral was reserved for worship. A vintage limousine pulled up in the forecourt of the cathedral to drop off a couple for the Sunday service. Another limousine circled around the statue of an earlier Queen in front of St Paul's Cathedral. It was my first glimpse of pageantry in London. I wanted to orientate myself in the new town. So I took a walk towards the Monument after beholding St Paul's Cathedral from the outside. The road seemed empty except for a few cars which drove past at great speed. No one could be seen walking along this road. I wondered about the absence of city-dwellers on a Sunday morning. Wanting to ask someone for directions, I approached a man walking at a distance in the opposite direction. He said that he didn't live in London. He was from Boston in Massachusetts, but he knew where Monument was. When I reached it, I was glad to see a group of tourists surrounding this Doric column.

I visited the City again after living in the wilderness for ten years, in North-West London. The City felt insular now, just as it did before. I had traversed the City by bus once or twice during these years. I made the mistake of boarding a bus one morning. When the bus reached Poultry, it was engulfed by a river of people gushing forth from the Underground. It was quicker to walk than to wait for the tide to subside. A few men rode very small bicycles like street entertainers. I had finally met the occupants of the City, whom I had longed to see during my first visit. I thought the churches in the City were cleaned by stone-cleaners, whereas in fact they were washed by the rain. The soot on the exterior of these buildings had been removed many years ago, causing consternation among Londoners.

I wanted to see Zack, who worked for a financial company in the City. I had met him five years before, when he had finished his degree course at the London School of Economics. His real name was Zakir, but his friends called him Zack. He was looking for a job in the City in those days. I remembered him buying a dark-grey suit at Cecil Gee for a job interview. He was looking for a room to rent around Somers Town near Euston, while hunting for a job and living with his parents in Hounslow. His father owned a hardware shop in Ealing. He had been to Harrow – an expensive fee-paying school – because his father wanted him to have a good education. His father was himself a semi-literate person. Zack spoke in the accent and tone of a Harrow School pupil.

I went to see Zack in the City during lunchtime. The City workers were grabbing sandwiches from the shops for lunch. We walked down the road, looking for somewhere to sit, until we reached Threadneedle Street. Zack said that there was a coffee shop inside the Royal Exchange, and it was there we were seated by a waiter in a smart uniform. The coffee shop occupied the centre of a courtyard, which was surrounded by boutiques. I ordered coffee for both of us. A lady sitting at the next table was having a lobster for lunch. Zack said that he had recently bought a house in Crouch End. He had married a woman from the Czech Republic two years ago. I asked him if his parents approved of his tying the knot with someone from another culture. Zack said that his parents would have liked him to marry someone from his own culture and had become resentful that he hadn't been to see them for the last two years. Zack was the eldest son in the family, with a younger brother and a sister. It was like being a rebel in the family to marry someone against his father's wishes.

Zack had met his wife, Marketta, three years ago, when she worked in a flower shop in the City. He used to buy sunflowers from her for his Swedish girlfriend, who left him for another broker in the City. When his girlfriend left him, he felt that she took his life with her and he felt very low for many months. Then one day he met Marketta in an

Underground station. She asked him why he didn't buy flowers any more. She felt sorry for him when he told her the reason. He was moved by her kindness and he went back to the flower shop to ask her out. She worked very hard for the florist for very little money, delivering flowers to various addresses in the City throughout the day. Zack helped her to get a National Insurance number, and now she worked in Whittington Hospital for a better wage.

Zack blamed himself when his first girlfriend left him. He had been deeply in love with her, but he couldn't bring her home to meet his parents. Her friends also advised her against marrying Zack, telling her that he would make her change her religion. Zack came from a Pathan background, and Pathans had a reputation for being loyal to their own tribe. There was a lot being written in the newspapers in those days about the marriage of an Englishwoman to a cricketer who happened to be a Pathan. It was frightening for Zack's girlfriend to read the gloomy presentiments of journalists about this marriage. Zack did not show any characteristics of his Pathan ancestry. His school at Harrow had made him a thoughtful person. And his hair had turned grey even though he was only in his late twenties.

There were only a handful of Asians working in the City. One had to be colour-blind not to notice that most City workers were white. Zack said that it was his father's ambition to see him working in the City. He himself would have liked to work for the BBC. And most of the Asian pupils who went to Harrow with Zack chose either law or medicine as a career. The high street banks had recruited many Asians in recent years to take abuse from their disgruntled customers. However, posts in the Lombard Street headquarters of these banks were reserved for English gentlemen. Zack felt isolated working in the City, and sometimes wished that he worked elsewhere.

Zack wanted reconciliation with his family. But for the last two years they considered him dead. He hadn't invited them to attend his wedding; it would have been like adding insult to their injury. It was a small wedding attended by a few people whom Zack worked with in the City. Marketta didn't have many friends in London. Her parents had travelled from Prague to attend the wedding. They were Catholics, and they expected their daughter to marry in a catholic church. But it was a civil marriage. The couple went to Prague for their honeymoon. Zack felt melancholy there because of severing ties with his family, especially as Marketta had been keen to get to know them. She had met his uncle a few times, and he seemed very nice to her. He was the only person who came to see them now and again. Marketta would have liked to meet Zack's sister, whom she heard was sweet. She could never cease thinking that it was because of her that Zack had been cast off by his family. The couple decided to return early from their honeymoon in Prague.

To be a worker in the City is to be a loner. It is a soulless place, like Christopher Wren's cathedral at its centre.

Wren also designed many parish churches in the City. These churches look like sham façades in an abandoned theatre. The numerous churches in Las Vegas are at least frequented by gamblers in order to confess their sins. Zack said that despite its pride in its wealth, the City, at heart, felt alien, like a poorhouse. He could not find a place among the City workers who met in the pubs during lunchtime. Every day he waited in his modern office for the evening so he could get out of the confines of the City. It gave him pleasure to pass Fetter Lane on his way home. The street name reminded me of the gangsters who called wives their 'ball and chain'. Zack was glad that his wife didn't work for the City florist any more. I was curious to know the reason for the omission of the family name 'Khan' on Zack's business card. He said that the name 'Khan' had associations that were frowned upon in the City. While hunting for a job, he found that he got a better response when his family name was misspelt as 'Kahn' on his curriculum vitae.

Thomas Gresham had built the first Royal Exchange in the middle of the sixteenth century. Business schools were established in the City around that time to teach their pupils the double-entry method of bookkeeping. Taking interest on loans was illegal in those days, but the law was generally evaded. We left Royal Exchange towards the eastern side to be greeted by the colossus of Paul Julius Reuter, wearing big whiskers. He began by bringing stock exchange prices by pigeon-post from Brussels to Aix-la-Chapelle, outpacing the mails, to the advantage of his clients. Reuter opened a small telegraph office in Royal Exchange in 1851 to gather share-market intelligence and international news. Its office building in Fleet Street was designed by Edwin Lutyens in 1935 after planning the Viceroy's House in New Delhi, which is one of the most monumental British buildings since Christopher Wren's St Paul's Cathedral.

As we turned into Threadneedle Street, Zack identified the Bank of England building for me. I had known it only in the subterranean name 'Bank' until then, without ever catching a glimpse of what it looked like overground. This Neoclassical structure does not announce its name to the passer-by. On inspection, one finds two structures – a new one superimposed on the old. The outer walls are that of the old Bank of England designed by Sir John Soane, who was a collector of artefacts and Egyptian sarcophagi. The new building, erected in the 1930s, was designed by Herbert Baker who had done some work in planning New Delhi on the recommendation of Edwin Lutyens. Baker had also worked under the patronage of Cecil Rhodes and was given numerous commissions for houses and churches in South Africa. Baker's bank is characterized by its imperial style, monumental in scale and reminiscent of his work in India.

Zack told me that banking in England was started by goldsmiths who gave loans to merchants and the Crown. They exchanged a handwritten receipt for the gold deposited with them. These receipts circulated freely, and as they promised to pay the bearer the sum as a form of paper money, they were the forerunners of banknotes. The merchants relied on Italians from Lombardy, who settled here in the twelfth century, for their accounting skills. The Sephardi Jewish families, who were mostly merchants and bankers, arrived in the City during the sixteenth century after fleeing the Inquisition in Spain and Portugal. They built a synagogue here, perhaps designed by Wren, who didn't want to attach his signature to it.

After passing the Lord Mayor's Mansion House, we took a stroll towards Cheapside. A Street sign had 'Old Jewry' written on it. I was baffled by this street name during my first visit to the City. I discovered later that this had been the Jewish quarter until Edward I expelled the entire community in the thirteenth century, and Judaism was banned in England for the next four hundred years.

I caught sight of a magnificent porch at a distance, which I thought was a church, but Zack told me it was the Guildhall – headquarters of the Corporation of London. I made a detour to see its Great Hall. Security was tighter here than at other City institutions, so tight that it was like going through airport security checks. There were metal detectors and X-ray machines installed in the corridor of the Great Hall. It reminded me of St George's Hall at Windsor, in which banquets were held for the Knights of the Garter. The banners of twelve City Livery Companies hung high over the frieze. These worshipful companies included those of

Goldsmiths, Mercers and Vintners. The oak-panelled roof was decorated with shields bearing the arms of the City Livery Companies, which were granted monopolies of trade during the time when monopoly was a legal term. The Great Hall was surrounded by monuments commemorating the victories of Nelson and Wellington. A minstrels' gallery guarded by pagan giants – Gog and Magog – overlooked the hall.

The hall was being set up for a banquet. The circular tables were laid over with textured beige cloths. A candelabrum stood on top of a round mirror at the centre of each table, and flower arrangements were displayed. The leather chairs had the crest of the Corporation of London stamped on them. The catering staff were arranging cutlery, glasses and napkins, folded in bishop's hat style, on the tables. It was here in the Guildhall that ceremonies were held to grant the Freedom of the City to visiting dignitaries. These ceremonies are still re-enacted now and again. Lawyers argued in the eighteenth century that every Englishman had a right to freedom of trade except in so far as it was limited by act of parliament and reasonable custom. Today, one can become a Freeman by patrimony or redemption – the payment on application, sponsored by two liverymen.

The medieval crypt of the Guildhall was closed, so we left the building straight after our look at the Great Hall. The shops along Cheapside bear no likeness to the canopied shop-fronts of the early twentieth century. These days, it boasts businesses like American Express Travel Services for the City bankers. At a street corner, a City gent was getting his shoes polished, and a tramp was doing push-ups nearby on the pavement. The big coaches brought hordes of tourists to St Paul's Cathedral. A new office block had been erected on the northern side of the cathedral. Zack said that the construction of office blocks in the city had continued since the nineteen-eighties, even though there was a lack of occupants to fill them, and some of the new buildings had been empty for many years. On reaching Postman's Park, I tried in vain to locate the postal museum, which I had found here during my first visit. It had disappeared in the intervening years. A narrow road near the park was named Little Britain.

I was disorientated when I visited the Barbican for the first time a few years ago to find its Arts Centre. I had entered a maze of passageways via a spiral staircase. I saw flats made of concrete as far as the eye could see, with very high tower blocks rising inside its perimeter. One of the towers was named after Thomas More, who was wrongfully charged with treason and beheaded in the nearby Tower of London. Thomas More's book was called *Utopia*, but the Barbican was an urban dystopia. A sixteenth-century church surrounded by the stagnant water of artificial lakes appeared in front of the Barbican Centre. John Milton – the blind poet who composed *Paradise Lost* – was buried in the church. The solitary figure of an elderly lady was walking towards the Arts Centre, a dismal location, which houses a concert hall, two theatres and a repertory cinema. Zack told me on my second visit that the Barbican is where the residents of the City live in tower blocks. I had confused the place with the retirement homes for reclusive artists who grew flowers on the ledges. The Barbican has remained true to the low Latin origins of its name, which means a fortified outpost.

We walked into the Arts Centre through its waterside entrance. I had forgotten what the building looked like from the inside. I had seen an overlong Shakespearian tragedy in one of the theatres a few years ago. When the play finished at 11pm, I found it difficult to find my way to the nearest tube station. Pedestrians were advised to follow yellow line routes painted on the ground to gain access to and from the Barbican, just as the painted line on the floor of a labyrinthine building leads one to the lifts. Sometimes, I would pick up a booklet of events at the Arts Centre from a library, and find something interesting to see there, but its location discouraged me from going there. In the 1950s City planners wanted to build a genuine residential neighbourhood to populate it again after the War, and their plan was endorsed by the Corporation of London, which took pride in their achievement. An arts centre was opened two decades later to put some life into this depressing estate.

Reflecting on his life as a financial adviser in the City, Zack said that there was no humanity in this soulless area. He could never forgive his father for sending him to the London School of Economics. Some of Zack's relatives were not happy either for him to work in the City. They were against usury and life insurance policies. At the LSE Zack believed that to be a City banker didn't mean that one had to be an astute person. He was an idealist, interested at the time in the left-wing economics of people like John Kenneth Galbraith. He felt demoralized after advising his clients on money matters. They were wealthy people looking for high dividends on their investments. He discovered an old alliance between the Crown, Parliament and City banks. It was William the Conqueror who had conferred a special status on the City, which is why they don't like to call him 'the Conqueror' in the City. The Bank of England had in fact played an important role in financing the war between Britain and France in the nineteenth century.

Zack said that when he was at college he believed financial independence would bring him happiness and self-esteem, and he could do whatever he wanted without seeking his father's approval. He thought money brought security and fulfilment. However, his job had taught him otherwise. He had found that the people he advised on financial matters were more insecure than those who weren't well off. Sometimes, his life in the City, in which every pleasure had to be paid for without even being enjoyed, filled him with a sad loathing. Then he would leave his office and take a walk towards Whitechapel and spend some time in the market. He had made friends with one or two traders there and he stopped at their stalls for a chat. It gave him more pleasure to visit the market than to go to a coffee shop in the City. Zack envied his grandfather for living a pastoral life in the Hindu Kush mountains.

Zack had grown up in a detached house in Isleworth. Having no contact with other children in the neighbourhood until he went to school, he used to play with the children at his father's shop in Ealing Broadway. The shop next door to his father's belonged to a Gujarati family who would also bring their children to the shop on the weekends. Zack looked forward to the weekends when his father would take him to the shop to play. Zack detested going to his school in Harrow which made him feel like an outsider. Most of the pupils came from rich families, who often went on holidays to exotic places. Zack's father kept his shop open seven days a week. The parents of other pupils invited each other to their homes. But Zack's mother could hardly speak English, and his parents never attended a parent's evening at the school. However, the tutors were happy with Zack's performance in class and wrote letters with appreciative remarks to his parents. As a youngster, Zack read Marx's treatise on capitalism. He never imagined that one day he would be working as a banker in the City. For some time, he became a person who shunned social gatherings. His classmates were into rock music and cult fiction. He loathed popular culture and turned into a recluse.

Zack felt embarrassed as a child when his parents spoke to each other in Pashtu in public places. Now he felt embarrassed that he could not speak Pashtu well. The things that were detestable to him then had become desirable to him now. He also disliked the food his mother cooked at home. He had never learnt how to cook while he was living with his parents. Sometimes, he cooked for his wife the way his mother used to, and Marketta loved it, even though he did not consider himself a good cook. Marketta could live on cereal and milk. She was not the kind of person who liked to eat out. Zack was critical of his parents for never eating in a restaurant. He did not attend office parties in the City, regarding them as displays of superficial hospitality. Without making any effort, he had become a pariah in the City.

I asked Zack about life outside his job. Zack told me that he had descended into a dark night of the soul since he had severed ties with his family. He felt that he was living a sterile life in Crouch End. Sometimes he took a lonely walk to Alexandra Palace to ponder over his desolate situation. When he reached its vantage point, a cold wind blowing on a fine day made it an inhospitable spot. Marketta didn't like to take a stroll in the park except during summer months. She watched soap operas on television to learn about the lives of her English neighbours, who did not care to greet her. It would take her more time to learn just how difficult it is to get to know one's neighbours in London. Marketta travelled to Prague once a year to see her folks. Zack hadn't travelled with her to Prague again since their honeymoon. She usually travelled by bus, packing food at home for her journey.

We left the Barbican Arts Centre by the main entrance, and took Long Lane towards Farringdon Road, where the company Zack worked for had its offices, housed in a glass and granite building stretching over a quarter of a mile. Zack bid me farewell and went back to his work. I walked towards Ludgate Circus to reach Fleet Street. I passed under a brightly-coloured iron bridge decorated with statues, known as Holborn Viaduct. I hadn't connected the name with this bridge, which I had passed under many times, until then. I turned into Fleet Street – a name to which many journalists and writers had paid homage in the last hundred years. I tried to locate the house of Samuel Johnson, who wore a wig and composed an English dictionary of 41,000 words. Many foreigners know more words in English these days than Dr Johnson knew in his lifetime. This house was hidden behind an alley way. The tradition of relying on hackwork in Fleet Street goes back to the time Johnson wrote *Rasselas* in one week to raise money for the funeral of his mother. A pair of street clocks loomed large over Fleet Street. Perhaps these clocks chimed the happy hour for the journalists working there during its heyday, or perhaps the clockmakers as a City Livery Company wanted to show off their craftsmanship. The Old Bell Tavern was already crowded before dusk. And close by was the entrance of Sergeant's Inn.

I had been there a long while ago with a friend to meet a barrister regarding a court case. His solicitor had arranged their meeting with his barrister a day before the hearing. English law didn't allow him to approach a barrister directly. It was a case between him and the City of Westminster, which wouldn't grant him permission to operate his business in the borough. The barrister was an Englishman who had studied law at Oxford. He was not too optimistic about the outcome of the case and wanted his client to withdraw before the hearing. But the client agreed to bear all legal charges, including those incurred by the City of Westminster, in case he lost the case. I went to Westminster City Hall the next day to witness the drama. The courtroom was on the seventeenth floor, with a good view of Buckingham Palace. The City of Westminster had a strong case, but the barrister produced such a fantastic argument against the objections of Westminster Council that the judge decided the case in favour of his client, who had paid his barrister £2,000 in advance as a fee.

I found a few bookshops along Fleet Street selling only legal books for barristers to help them in litigation. Many of these legal books were published by Her Majesty's Stationery Office. A group of cameramen were waiting outside the Old Bailey as usual to take pictures of whoever was on trial that day. They had mounted empty coffee cups on the spikes of a fence like the heads of the traitors that were displayed here until the mid-eighteenth century. The City ended here, and beyond Temple Bar was the City of Westminster. The Monarch has to ask for the Lord Mayor's permission to enter the City, just as Salvador Dali needed written permission from his wife to enter his own house. But a commoner is free to enter the City without such permission.

Fleet Street was a centre of book publishing before its association with the newspaper industry. It was here that the books of Thomas More and Francis Bacon were published for the first time. A pupil of William Caxton had moved printing presses from Westminster to Fleet Street at the beginning of the sixteenth century. Caxton had acquired the art of printing during his sojourn in Cologne, two decades after Gutenberg had printed his Bible using movable type. Caxton was diligent in practising his craft and the labour of translation. His apprentice moved the Caxton presses to Fleet Street to be close to the lawyers who were his customers. The other booksellers also founded printing houses in Fleet Street around that time, and a number of bookbinders established themselves near the printing houses.

The names of long-vanished newspapers survive today on the walls of the buildings in Fleet Street. It is because of these newspapers that Fleet Street has entered the lexicon as an incarnation of British journalism. For some reason, I had also associated the name Fleet Street with yellow journalism. I had heard this street name before I arrived in London, but the street seemed quieter than I had imagined it and I wondered if there was more than one Fleet Street in London. At the time I hadn't realized that the newspaper offices had moved elsewhere. I carried in my mind a picture of Fleet

Street painted by an artist in 1930. In that picture, the pavements were crowded with pedestrians, whilst old red and black buses travelled up and down. A steam locomotive crossed an overhead bridge. The rising steam mingled with other fumes to create a haze, which enveloped the dome of St Paul's Cathedral. Words such as 'news', 'daily' and 'papers' were inscribed on the walls in sepia ink. My impression of Fleet Street was out of date. I visited it more than sixty years after the artist had captured it on his canvas. What had happened in the intervening years to cause the street to change its character so conspicuously?

A few weeks later, I phoned Zack at home to express my gratitude to him for showing me the City. He invited me to join him and his wife for lunch that day in a riverside café near London Bridge. I agreed to meet them at one o'clock on the other side of the bridge. In the Strand I waited for a bus outside Coutts – the Queen's bank. I boarded a number 15 towards Aldgate. When I asked the conductor where I should get off for London Bridge, he asked me if I meant Tower Bridge. Perhaps people visiting London mistakenly referred to Tower Bridge as London Bridge. The friendly West Indian conductor said that the number 15 was used by many tourists for sightseeing because it followed a historical route. After this chat, he said that I should get off at Bank to get to London Bridge. As the bus struggled to drive up Ludgate Hill, the conductor reminded me to get off at the next stop before the bus reached Bank. He also told me that

King William Street leads to London Bridge. I took a walk across it. The new footbridge on the right-hand side was busy with lovers of modern art on their way to the Tate Modern. Two elderly Pearly Kings stood on the other side of the bridge, attracting the attention of passers-by. During Victorian times, the costermongers elected their own King, who wore clothes studded with myriads of pearl buttons. The bridge resounded with the amplified voices of the tour guides on cruise boats passing under it. One of the guides mentioned to his audience that one of the glass-fronted buildings along the riverside had perhaps been designed by a window cleaner.

On my way to Tooley Street, I found a very long queue of people standing by railway arches. Some of them were dressed in black, and had also dyed their hair black. I walked past the queue to find out what was housed inside the railway arches. The entrance to the vaults was guarded by doormen who wore hooded cloaks and had their faces painted white. It was the London Dungeon, where Jack the Ripper was resurrected and the Great Fire of London burned forever like the fire in a Zoroastrian temple. The grown-ups waiting in a long queue to get in were seemingly fascinated by the macabre.

I finally found the Galleria where I was to meet Zack. An eighteenth-century ship was docked there for ornamental purposes. A few joggers were running along the riverside, but many people were taking a leisurely walk towards Tower

Bridge. I sat down on a bench to watch the panorama of the City on the other side of the river.

A few minutes later, Zack arrived with his wife. Marketta, who was slightly taller than Zack, had thin hair and a round face. She wore make-up like a thin mask. Marketta spoke English affectedly. When I asked her if she was happy working for the NHS, she answered in a supercilious way. The waiter came to take our order. I ordered a sandwich, and Marketta ordered a starter and a main course. Zack was content with a Spanish omelette. Marketta had been for a job interview at Guy's Hospital that morning. She was looking for a better job within the NHS. Because she lacked the experience required for such an interview, Zack had prepared her for it. He had advised her to show her passion about the job to the interviewer so that he didn't think she was only interested in the money. Marketta said that her interview had gone well and she was hopeful about its outcome. I wanted to express my gratitude to Zack by paying the bill for our lunch, but he insisted that I was his guest.

I asked Marketta about her life in London before she met Zack. She said that City gentlemen had often offered her work in their companies when she worked for a florist. But it didn't take her long to realize that they wanted something from her in return. Since she was a foreign waitress, all the male customers wanted to know if she had a boyfriend or if she was living on her own. They saw her as someone gullible and therefore easy to seduce. Many married men wanted her to be their mistress. One of the men even made her believe that a certain woman was his business partner, though in fact she was his wife. It was part of her growing up to work as a flower seller in the City. Some of the girls from her part of the world had fallen into the vagaries of affluence in London. They paid a membership fee to a gym, when they had no money to pay their rent. That is where married men became helpful. Marketta said that she was lucky to find Zack, who was unlike the other men she had met in the City, men of dubious trustworthiness. She thought it was unlikely that she would have found another job without selling her soul.

What did Marketta think of Zack's family, who hadn't accepted her? She said that she knew that the reason for her husband's melancholy was the bitterness of his family. Zack had felt for many months that the world outside his family home in Hounslow was unwelcoming. She felt that they were like two outcasts, leaning on each other for mutual support. I remembered him being a cheerful person when I first met him, but Zack's mood hadn't changed since leaving his family home. Marketta had thought that Zack's family would eventually forgive him and accept her as their daughter-in-law. But they had lived up to their tribal reputation, and they considered him dead. She said that she would like to move to another European country with Zack. Perhaps the diversion would lessen his sense of loss. He had lost weight in the last two years. Working in the City filled him with dread.

Abuja to London

Walking down Swallow Street one evening, I was nodded to by a doorman as I passed the entrance of the restaurant where he stood. He wore the formal attire of a doorman – top hat, long coat, white shirt and tie. He looked well-groomed and he had a cheerful countenance. I often passed this quiet side-street on my way to work, and had developed a nodding acquaintance with the doorman, stopping for small talk like 'How's business?' now and again. He earned a minimal wage, but some of the patrons of the restaurant gave him a tip when he hailed a taxi for them. Therefore, he liked it when the restaurant was busy. The days it wasn't busy, he went home with only his basic wage.

Solomon had come to London from Abuja in Nigeria five years ago. His father had moved to Abuja twenty-six years earlier when a new city was being built at the site of the old town. The new city was designed by a Japanese architect on a grand scale. The need for a new capital was felt after the discovery of oil in Nigeria in the nineteen-sixties. Solomon's father owned a small business in Abuja. When he was a child, he remembered the town as a building site. The city took shape as he grew up. His father belonged to the Anglican Church, and Solomon attended the service with him every Sunday. His parents spoke Yoruba, but he was taught English at school. Solomon got married in Abuja at the age of eighteen, and five years later he married again in London. He had a boy and a girl with his first wife and two boys with the second wife. When I asked him if the Anglican Church permitted a man to have two wives, he said that the church never 'unpermitted' a man to have more than one wife. He sent money every month to his wife in Abuja for bringing up his children, and he worked hard to feed and clothe his other two children in London. He worked six days a week, twelve hours a day, as a doorman, earning just enough to keep his head above water. On Sundays he went to a church for Nigerians.

It took Solomon four years to find a doorman job in London. He had done many odd jobs before applying for this position. He lived in a dormitory in Willesden during his first year, where he paid £40 a week for accommodation. As a black person, Solomon found it very difficult in the beginning to find any kind of work in London. Employers were mistrustful of his nationality. The first job he found was that of a pot washer in a restaurant kitchen. It was casual work; the restaurant manager called him whenever he needed him. Sometimes he worked two days a week, sometimes four. Solomon was still looking for a regular job when he met a door-to-door salesman who offered him work. To look presentable as a salesman, he bought a new suit from the money he had saved. He was told that those Londoners who have seen Arthur Miller's play, *Death of a Salesman*, sometimes take pity on a person who knocks at their door and buy what he has to offer. The next morning, Solomon was given a list of homes in a certain area where he would try to sell British Gas. He didn't have much luck. Someone told him a couple of weeks later that he wouldn't make it as a door-to-door salesman in London. He went back to pot washing the following week.

Solomon approached many Asians who ran small businesses in London for a job. Their answer was that they were running a family business only. Most of these Asians had come from Africa, but they had no sympathy for Africans, regarding any who walked into their shop with suspicion and telling their staff to keep a sharp eye on them. Solomon thought of going back to Abuja, but his return ticket had expired and he couldn't raise the money to buy a new ticket. Only his Sunday churchgoing gave him some consolation during those difficult days. He knew it was only in the Bible that he could find help in time of need: 'Dear friends, do not be surprised at the painful trial you are suffering, as though something strange were happening to you. But rejoice that you participate in the sufferings of Christ' (1 Peter 4:12). Solomon always carried a pocket-sized Bible with him. He would read a passage from it whenever he felt depressed or discouraged. He also found a few friends among the people who attended Sunday service with him. Without their support, Solomon said, he would have ended up in a mental hospital.

The next job Solomon found was standing on the pavement in a High Street, holding a signboard pointing towards a business in a side-street. Autumn had just set in and it was getting cold. After a month, he felt the chill in his bones from standing in a cold wind for ten hours a day. He could carry on only until the end of October. Luckily he found a temporary job as a security guard in a footwear shop in Regent Street until Christmas that year. He was paid cash in hand in his previous jobs, but he required a bank account for this new job. He found that banks were reluctant to open an account for him. The Royal Bank of Scotland told him that he should try the National Westminster Bank near where he lived; but he didn't have the necessary utility bills in his name, because he lived in a dormitory. He was introduced to Barclays Bank by a friend who was an account holder. They refused to open an account for him, stating that the person who had introduced him to the bank was not creditworthy because he had once exceeded his credit limit by £10. Finally, after two months of refusals, the Hong Kong and Shanghai Bank was kind enough to open an account for Solomon.

His temporary job contract came to an end after Christmas. However, the company was looking for someone on a permanent basis to fill his position. Solomon applied as a candidate for the job. Asked to provide two sound references in support of his application, he gave the name of his Anglican priest as one of his referees. Solomon was also told that the candidate should have a clean driving licence. He could not see the connection between a driving licence and being a security guard. Since he didn't have a licence, he was turned down as a candidate for the job, which he had performed well for three months. He took the Bible from his pocket and opened it at random. On that page was a call to persevere. Walking aimlessly along Regent Street one day, he went into the shoe shop he had worked in six weeks earlier to say hello to a sales assistant. When the manager saw him, he said that he wanted to have a chat with him and asked if he could come back tomorrow. Solomon thought that it was regarding a matter when he worked there.

He went back the next day to see the manager, who asked him if he was still looking for a job. Apparently, the shop had gone through two security guards in six weeks. The first one was sacked after a month because he was doing nothing to prevent the theft of shoes from the shop. The second one failed to turn up after two weeks. Solomon accepted the job with a feeling of great relief to be employed full-time. He discovered the benefits of a regular job, which were unknown to him previously. He was entitled to four weeks holiday a year, but he decided to cash in the holidays instead. He was paid a weekly wage of £176. He sent £100 every two weeks to his wife in Abuja through Western Union. It cost him another £20 by way of transmission fee. He spent £65 on his accommodation and travelling, which left £50 a week for food, clothes and entertainment.

Solomon found other Africans living in London, who wore gold ornaments like costume jewellery. They played at fruit machines and entertained women in various bars and pubs. He wondered about their private income, by virtue of which they entertained women without making any effort. He felt tempted by the more wholesome women who walked into the shop, some of whom were friendly to him. He was unsure whether it was his khaki uniform or the colour of his skin which attracted them. Besides, he was living a hand-to-mouth existence and it was beyond his scope to court these women.

However, he met a woman in church during Advent that year, and they were married by Easter. Stella was from Lagos, and Solomon told her about his first wife in Abuja who had been refused a visa to join her husband in London by the British High Commission. Solomon said that his marriage to Stella saved him from a life of temptation and sin. The Anglican priest who declared the couple man and wife also knew about Solomon's first wife and children, but, astonishingly, he was so sympathetic to him that he ignored this fact.

The couple rented a room in Kilburn after the wedding. Stella worked as a cleaner in a few offices and banks until she was eight months pregnant. She gave up her job three weeks before the birth of a baby boy. Solomon, who had desperately missed his children in Nigeria for two years, was exhilarated at the birth of a new baby. He took up part-time work as well, because his wife could not go to work any more. Solomon had informed his wife in Abuja about his second marriage, but promised to send her money as usual. Stella gave birth to another son fifteen months later. Solomon could not spend any time with her because he came home late from work. He usually brought home tins of milk for his children. On the days he worked even later, his children went without milk. Stella was patient with him because she understood that Solomon had two families to feed. A woman of generous disposition, she didn't mind that he sent money to his first wife twice a month. The church had taught her to be generous and she believed in forgiveness.

Meanwhile, the restaurant in Swallow Street changed hands and the new owners were looking for a friendly doorman to help promote the business. The new manager of the restaurant usually bought his shoes from the shop where Solomon worked and since Solomon had once told him that he was looking for another job, the new manager sent him a message to come and see him. Would he be interested in working as a doorman for his restaurant? It was a very well-known restaurant, which attracted lots of customers. The manager told him that he would earn only the minimum wage as a doorman, but he could keep tips for himself.

Solomon accepted the job, hoping to earn a bit more than what he earned as a security guard. It took him a few months to get to know the regular customers who would look after him when they left the restaurant. But he enjoyed chit-chat with the customers waiting to be seated whenever the restaurant was very busy. As he improved in carrying out his duties as a doorman, he received more gratuities from the patrons of the restaurant. Solomon said that a doorman always remembers two types of people – those who are generous in their kindness to him and those who never show their gratitude. He would acknowledge the former and ignore the latter. He relied on the kindness of strangers for his living. Before he took up his office, the Mayor of London also came to dine at the Swallow Street restaurant every few weeks. On leaving the restaurant after having a meal, Solomon would always offer to flag a cab for him when he left. But the mayor replied that he would like to take a walk and then jump into a cab further down the street.

Solomon learned more about another culture by working as a doorman than by living in a multi-cultural neighbourhood. The English businessman who came to the restaurant with his mistress one week would come to the same place with his wife and children the next. In fact, he claimed to be a loving father and husband who envied Solomon for having two wives – one in Abuja and one in London. He had warned Solomon not to confuse his wife with his mistress. The gentleman, who owned a market in

East London, was very prosperous. Other men told Solomon that it was expensive enough for them to maintain a wife, never mind a mistress who was beyond their means. The businessman sometimes treated his mistress's entire family to a three-course meal in the Swallow Street restaurant, where the price of a meal was very high. Solomon liked the market owner, because he was a very considerate person.

This was his only social life, engaging in small talk as a doorman. I asked him what it was like for him when he first arrived in London from Abuja.

'I felt like a squatter living outside Abuja', he said, 'who is excluded from the goings-on of the federal capital territory. I saw the frightening faces of Africans selling marijuana at street corners, living on the fringes of society. Their only dealings with that society were to supply its misfits with narcotics to render them insensible. They offered ganja to me as well, every time I passed a certain road. It was the Nigerian church in London that offered me sanctuary in the beginning from the horrors outside and made me feel welcome. I passed a hospital on my way to church in those days. Sometimes, I would come across a few of its patients from psychiatric wards taking a walk outside the hospital. There were a few Africans among them. One of them took a brisk walk with bare feet and unbuttoned shirt in the middle of winter. He always carried an umbrella with him. I feared for my mental health if I didn't go to church regularly. I had left a family behind in Abuja, and I had no one to talk to in

London. The bleakness of winter in London filled me with despair. I had enjoyed going to a park in summer to fill my spare time, but I longed to go back to Abuja during the winter. My father had suffered losses in his business, and he had fallen on hard times. I thought that it was better to bear cold than to be a coward. I spent my first winter in an unheated room.'

What did he think of those of his countrymen who were living lavishly in London?

'I am not surprised to see them staying at Claridge's. But I am shocked to see how much money they spend on clothes and pointless accessories in the West End. Sometimes the shopkeepers carry the shopping for them in their own cars to the hotels where they are staying in Mayfair. Nigeria is an oil-exporting country, and the proceeds from exports mainly benefit the chieftains and those who run the government. They come to London very often to spend their money. Sometimes, they also bring their clothes with them to be dry-cleaned in London. Fifty years ago, we would have blamed the colonial rulers for sapping the country. But today we have Nigerians in charge of the country. Those people in Nigeria who aspire to get rich very quickly send letters to people all over the world saying that they have millions of dollars from the proceeds of oil exports, which they would like to transfer to an overseas account. They offer the overseas account holder a cut. Some of the people, who are overcome with greed, give out their account details. A few of them are foolish enough to pay the charges beforehand, only to find out that it is a trick. There are also men in Lagos who buy merchandise in various countries with a Letter of Credit from a bank in Nigeria. When the merchandise is shipped to Lagos, the bank does not honour their Letter of Credit.'

How did he reconcile himself to a society which had lost its Christian values?

'I am surprised to find that Christianity has withered away in England. My ancestors converted to Christianity due to the missionary work of Anglican priests in Africa. After arriving in London, I saw that the churches in every neighbourhood had fallen into disuse, or some of them were used for other purposes. I saw mostly Africans going to church on Sundays, looking colourful in their national costumes. Christianity seems like a religion of less affluent Londoners. I feel that Christianity went into decline in Britain with the loss of the empire. Those Africans who bring their laundry with them to London also carry a copy of the Bible. The only place I have seen the Bible over here is in the drawer of the bedside table in a hotel room. I have heard people in England calling a *Baedeker* the Bible. I have found very few Christian values in practice in this society. On the contrary, we are being taught gluttony and envy.'

Had he become colour-conscious after living in London for the last few years?

'The West Indians living in London look down on Africans, even though we are the same colour. I cannot think of any other city in Europe as cosmopolitan as London. But English folks mostly keep themselves to themselves. I do not engage in greetings with others outside work, in case they think I am trying to be familiar. My uncle in Abuja married a Russian woman when he was a student at the Patrice Lumumba University in Russia. I was fascinated by the very light colour of my cousins. I had hardly seen people of another colour in Abuja as a child. Whenever we saw a man of another colour as children, we would gather around that person. Abuja was not like Kenya where the white tourists ventured out so often on safaris. Those tourists were warned by their Foreign Offices not to go to Nigeria, which was considered a dangerous country to travel in. When I went to Nairobi once with my father, I thought that I had reached another continent. I liked it when I arrived in London because I could find people from every country in the world living in this city. Regent Street appeared to me as a confluence of many races. I don't think that I would feel comfortable living in Somerset or Dorset.'

Solomon said that his only extravagance was to buy a fancy pair of shoes now and again. It was an African predilection for him to wear crocodile shoes. He told me that the pair he wore was made in Africa from real crocodile skin. I had thought that those shoes were called crocodile shoes because of their shape. They were expensive, whether you bought them in Lagos or London. Solomon had only a few pairs here, but he had many pairs in Abuja. I was not sure if it was legal to make shoes from crocodile skin but Solomon said that one could breed crocodiles and use their skin for that purpose.

Solomon had moved to a one-bedroom flat in Tottenham a few months before I met him. He rented the flat from an Asian landlord who owned a few houses in the area. The Asians would have him as a tenant in the end, but he had found it very difficult to be employed by them in the beginning. London cabbies generally refused a fare to Tottenham which was a black neighbourhood. I had been through the area a few times on my way to Tottenham Hale. After passing Manor House, the road offered a prospect of grim council flats. The estate gave way to small houses and a clutter of shops. A few men in Rastafarian gear stood at the entrance of a tube station. The inspectors, who were checking commuters for tickets, were guarded by policemen standing nearby. As I turned into the High Road, a few more policemen could be seen on the beat. The High Road was busy, with many buses running along this route. I turned into West Green Road at the next intersection, and it joined Green Lanes with High Road. There were many Halal butchers along this road who sold low grade meat at cheap prices. There were also a number of greengrocers run by Turkish men and women. The other shops were like general stores, selling their wares at discounted prices, mostly household goods like plastic roses and rugs made of synthetic material.

It was in a flat above the shops that Solomon lived. He told me that some of these flats were so rundown that their landlords couldn't find tenants and they had been empty for some time.

Why didn't London cabbies accept fares to Tottenham?

'It is because they think it's highly dangerous for them to take a passenger to Tottenham, which is a black neighbourhood like Brixton. But people don't come to our neighbourhood to buy drugs. If you want, you can readily find drugs in Bloomsbury. In fact, the drugs business in Tottenham is controlled by the Turkish gangs who operate from the back rooms of grocery shops in Green Lanes in an old-fashioned way. They sell drugs to the black men to keep them downtrodden. I feel as safe living in Tottenham as in any other neighbourhood in London. I am afraid of going to Millwall at night. I have heard from various people that when they came down to London from the Midlands in the nineteen-fifties, one could hardly see a black face in London. They also say that you could leave your front door open then with no fear of burglary. I once got stopped by a policeman on the road who told me that he was not spiteful. Perhaps he was conscious of spitefulness in his department towards the black population. Elderly people in London are not frightened of Chinese gangs, who are more ruthless than any others, but they are afraid of a big African man walking in the street. I am myself of small stature – I don't find much discrimination against me. A hundred years ago, an African scholar wrote letters to his masters in Great Britain begging for their patronage. But times have changed and we live in an emancipated world.'

A Kiosk in
Charing Cross Road

When I first saw Kasim at his kiosk, he was giving directions to a couple who wanted to get to Sadler's Wells. He told them it was five 'bounds' by taxi. For the next few weeks, I thought that a 'bound' was a unit of measurement in colloquial English, like a furlong. Then I heard Kasim quoting prices in 'bounds' to his customers, and I realized that he was unable to say 'pound'. There is no consonant corresponding to the sound of the English 'p' in Arabic, so it was replaced by the sound 'b'. He must have tried in the beginning to produce the unfamiliar sound and then given up on it or maybe he didn't know himself that he had replaced one consonant with another. A few years later, I heard a joke going around in London about an Arab motorist who asks an Englishman, 'Where can I "bark", sir?' The Englishman replies, 'This is a free country. You can "bark" wherever you like.'

One evening, when I passed the kiosk as usual, I found Kasim picking up his broken glasses and spilled chocolates from the floor. His teeth and lips were bleeding and his shirt was ripped. He had been beaten up by a bunch of youths, who had taken chocolates and drinks from the shelves. Kasim did not bother to call the police, because he knew that it meant paperwork for him and only a letter of apology from the police. The kids had run away with their spoils and it was very difficult to catch them. Besides, they were too young to be given a custodial sentence for looting a kiosk. Kasim was only running the kiosk for a wage from the owner, who would come every Saturday to collect the takings from him. The owner wouldn't learn about this incident when he came to see Kasim later that week. Every few days Kasim went to the Booker cash-and-carry at King's Cross in his car to buy cigarettes and drinks for the kiosk. He also maintained a cashbook, entering the weekly takings on one side and the receipts from the cash-and-carry on the other side. The difference between the two amounts was owed by him to the proprietor of the business. Many people believed that the kiosk belonged to Kasim, never having seen anybody else there.

Kasim came from a village in the Tala District of Egypt, which was also the birthplace of President Anwar Sadat. It was one of the backwaters of Egypt until Anwar Sadat came to power and he did much to bring modern facilities to the village. Kasim was working in Luxor when he met Pat from Penge in London, who was on a two-week holiday in Egypt. They fell in love and decided to marry during the same week. Their wedding took place in front of an Imam and two witnesses. Kasim was twenty-four years old. Pat was a 38-year-old divorcée with an eight-year-old daughter. It took Kasim six months to obtain the necessary visa to join his spouse in London. During those months Pat visited him again in Luxor where he toiled to save money for the journey to London. Pat was living in a council flat in Penge when Kasim eventually arrived. He was frowned upon by other tenants on the estate, who considered him to be a toyboy, a plaything for a middle-aged woman.

Pat's first husband also lived in the same estate. He was a tramp, who hung around outside a local liquor shop and laughed at Kasim every time he saw him walking down the road with Pat. At first Kasim ignored him but then he became embarrassed to see him. Kasim was lucky to find a job within a month of his arrival in London. He had picked up conversational English from the tourists in Luxor. He could not read and write English but he was endowed with a good memory, learning the names of things very quickly. He was also a trustworthy person. The Asian businessman who employed him was able to trust Kasim with running the business after a few months. This businessman owed a huge sum to Her Majesty's Customs and Excise and declared himself bankrupt to evade payment. His business was closed down and Kasim lost his job, soon after which Pat gave birth to Kasim's child. Kasim whispered 'Azan' into the right ear of the newborn baby and named him Ali after his grandfather.

Pat's relationship with Kasim began to falter when Ali was a year old. She started drinking again after two years. Kasim took a dislike to her for being alcoholic and wanted to run away from her. One day he boarded the train to Heathrow to leave the country, but he couldn't get a seat on the next flight to Cairo. Then he thought about his son, and took a train back to Penge.

The couple separated after living together for two years. Kasim found a room in Sydenham, where he worked in a fish-and-chips bar. He wore a white jacket and a paper cap while serving customers there. The bar was owned by a Greek-Cypriot who liked Kasim for his honesty and hard work. Pat wouldn't let Kasim see his son once a week until he paid her maintenance so he agreed to pay her £250 a month for the next five years. It had been seven years since they got divorced, and Kasim was still paying the money for the sake of his son. It took Kasim three years to get divorced from Pat, during which he became familiar with the procrastination of the English legal system. He met a fellow Egyptian in the Royal Courts of Justice who had been fighting a custody battle over his children for the last twelve years. The children were grown up now and no longer needed a custodian.

Kasim was planning to marry again, but this time to someone from his own village in Egypt. His family wanted to arrange it for him. They had mentioned Zeinab, a widow at twenty-five, whose husband had died just six months after their wedding. Kasim's family felt compassion for Zeinab, who found it very difficult as a widow to find a husband in Tala District. It was not easy either for Kasim, who had married a foreign woman in Luxor, to find a wife in his village. His family couldn't send him a photograph of Zeinab because they didn't consider it honourable to ask for the picture of a widow. They wanted Kasim to pay a visit to his village to see her. It was customary in their village to be as respectful of other families' daughters as one was respectful of one's own daughters. And prospecting for a bride was a sensitive affair. Kasim had once asked Saeed, a friend in Luxor, if Saeed had met the woman it had been arranged for him to marry after a few months. The friend replied in disbelief that he was not so low-class. Kasim considered himself fortunate that his family could arrange a marriage for him in Egypt as his chances of marrying in London were slim. Like a nineteenth century-traveller, Kasim thought that Englishwomen at home and Englishwomen abroad were different in character. He had often wondered at his own folly in marrying Pat in Luxor.

Kasim had taken over the running of the kiosk at Charing Cross Road eight years earlier. He found it exciting to work in Central London. Everyone looked like a tourist with a backpack and a street map in their hands. They stood at the crossroads looking for street signs. An orderly crowd gathered outside the Garrick Theatre every evening. Across the road, the Alhambra survived only in name. The building in grand Moorish style at this site had been replaced by a structure of iron and glass. A row of antiquarian bookshops looked picturesque in a precinct off Charing Cross Road. The second-hand bookshops on the main road looked dingy, but they seemed busier than the ones in Cecil Court. A notice in the window of one of these shops read 'Tomorrow our books will fly / From London to Hay on Wye'. The notice inside the shop warned browsers not to take their bags into the basement. The shop also gave a used carrier bag to whoever bought a book. When I asked the bookseller for a certain book, he replied that his shop was not a branch of Waterstone's where they could look up a title on a computer. He told me to go through the books on the shelves and see if I could find a copy there. It had been many years since Marks & Co. had closed down its famous bookshop at 84 Charing Cross Road. Mr Marks had felt disconcerted by the arrival of transistor radios and people listening to loud music on their portable radios. The age of romance between a bookseller and his customers had passed into history.

Fashion students worked till late dressing up mannequins on the first floor of St Martin's College of Art along this road. Some wag had inserted a 'T' and 's' on the signboard of the college, changing its name into 'Saint Martin's College of TArts'. I saw a group of passers-by captivated by the sight of acoustic guitars in a shop-window. A bookseller in one of the big bookshops here said that it was heart-rending for him to witness the homelessness along this road. The remaining few second-hand bookshops in Charing

Cross Road were disappearing one by one. However, the tobacco and snuff shop had survived for over a hundred years. The Presbyterian Church had been converted into a nightclub. But visitors to London attended concerts by candlelight in St Martin-in-the-Fields at the other end of the road. They also took part in the ritual of brass rubbing in the crypt of this church.

The kiosk had three-room tenement flats above it. Some of them were occupied by families and some by single people living in bedsits. All of them were foreigners, who mostly bought their confectionery from Kasim. One of them was a South African. She had red hair and a freckled face, and sometimes she would come downstairs without her shoes to buy a carton of milk. Kasim usually obliged by going across the road to buy milk for her. She had learnt how to say 'Thank you' in Arabic to Kasim. Among other patrons of the Kiosk was Gordon, a Scotsman, who spent half an hour every day in chit-chat with Kasim. He came from a small village in the Highlands but had lived alone for the past twenty years in Covent Garden and knew many people who were running small businesses around there. Gordon was an amiable person who had found companionship among foreigners. He was invited to the weddings of small traders and he always attended funerals. Unlike many Londoners, he understood the cultural differences between a Gujarati and a Bengali trader. He also helped these traders in understanding the meaning of official correspondence.

Having once worked for the City of Westminster as a clerk, he gave an insight into the clerical mind to Kasim, who received many official letters from the City of Westminster. The council wanted Kasim to change the front of his kiosk by replacing the shutter with a glass front, or risk its closure. However, the design had to be approved by the council. Gordon had found an architect for Kasim, who would submit his drawings to the council for approval. It had taken two years for the architect to get his drawings approved. The architect charged Kasim a fee of £1,000. The shop-fitter wanted £3,000 to make a new front. The kiosk was not making so much money that Kasim could afford such an expense, so he found an identical frame fitted with a glass door in a DIY store and paid a builder £200 to have it fitted. It cost him £2,000 in all to install a new kiosk front. A few months later, Kasim received another letter from the City of Westminster saying that the new front of the kiosk did not exactly conform to the drawing that had been approved by the council. He sought Gordon's help in drafting a letter to the Westminster Council.

It was Kasim's responsibility to deal with the council on behalf of the owner of the kiosk, who paid an instalment of the Business Rates for the kiosk at the end of each month. The owner had missed a monthly instalment in the past, and one day a huge man with ginger hair, smartly dressed in a suit and tie, appeared in the kiosk demanding the money. If refused, he threatened to take the goods and chattels instead.

He wouldn't accept a cheque, only cash or a credit card payment. He gave Kasim three hours to raise the money, which Kasim borrowed from a friend for a few days. He was unable to reach the owner of the kiosk, who came to collect the money from him every Saturday, on the phone. Since that day, when he became acquainted with a bailiff for the first time, Kasim remembered to pay the Business Rates on time. He had heard about this loathsome character, but never imagined he would be wearing a suit and tie.

Kasim traversed Leicester Square, where people gathered for entertainment in the evenings, on his way home. Sometimes the sound of pan-pipes, played by a group of men from the Andes who wore long hair, ponchos and hats, would lure him to join the bystanders and listen to the music for a few minutes. Another entertainer, who sang an Eagles song every night, passed the kiosk in the evening carrying his musical instruments. The street entertainer rolled up marijuana in a back-alley for a smoke before giving his performance. A row of cafés served global food. These cafés were run by Arab men, who asked every woman walking into their shop, 'Will you marry me?' in jest. A North African man followed an Englishwoman, saying, 'I want to have a conversation with you'. It was amusing for Kasim to watch these scenes played out. One evening he encountered a troupe of female performers in Bear Street. Their faces were painted white and they wore theatrical costumes. They undressed in Bear Street to get changed. It was as if mannequins were changing their clothes in front of the passers-by. Kasim liked to watch street theatre. It reinforced his idea of the essentially theatrical nature of London. However, he had never been inside the Garrick Theatre in all his years of trading in the same street. He was happy just to see a queue of theatre-goers outside his kiosk.

Kasim kept his kiosk open till late on the weekends, when he took more money than the rest of the week. He discovered that Central London changed its character during the night. People became sociable and exchanged greetings with strangers. It took him a few months to realize that it was the influence of alcohol which made Londoners so sociable after midnight. A double-decker hired by party-goers halted in front of the kiosk to drop off rowdy men and women from its top deck. A stretch limo drove by now and again, carrying a group of girls who played at being glamorous. A tramp touched up the chalked sketch of the Houses of Parliament on the pavement, drawn by him the night before with an inscription for the sweeper saying, 'Please do not remove'. The evening brought different people to the West End from those who came in daytime. A few of them were entertainers, and a multitude were those who liked to be entertained. Theatre actors walked down Charing Cross Road every evening incognito, but an occasional visit by a film star caused a stir.

One evening Kasim was looking melancholy when I stopped at his kiosk. He told me about his foreboding that the owner might give up the kiosk because the landlord was putting up the rent. The landlord also objected to keeping the kiosk open till midnight at weekends, and the council wanted higher rates for trading during the night. If the new terms of the landlord were accepted, the kiosk would turn into a loss-making unit. Kasim was worried about finding another job after running the kiosk independently for so many years. He didn't consider himself competent in looking for a new job, especially as he didn't have any computer skills. He was hoping that a compromise would be reached by the two parties. The landlord was represented by an estate agency, which didn't like to budge. The owner was ready to accept the higher rent, but the restriction on business hours was unacceptable. It was impossible to survive in business without keeping the kiosk open until midnight at the weekend. Kasim made a profit mostly by selling water and soft drinks to frolickers in the evening. He made very little money by selling cigarettes. It also meant a big investment for him to keep all the brands of cigarettes in stock. Therefore, he would buy cigarettes from a wholesaler in Soho every two days.

A number of pickpockets and shoplifters plied their trade on Charing Cross Road. They offered their pickings to Kasim for sale, but he always refused to partake in this business. Sometimes, it was those who had fallen on hard times offering their belongings for sale. A frail Englishman was trying to raise £50 for his marriage to a Ukrainian woman. He showed his paintings to Kasim at the kiosk. The Englishman, aged twenty-five, had fallen in love with the Ukrainian woman, who had a son of the same age. Kasim said that he was a collector of ruins when he heard this diffident Englishman's story, and bought one painting for £20 from him out of compassion. Kasim saw him again after a year. He had found a job as a car mechanic, and was living with his wife and her son. He told Kasim that it broke his heart that he couldn't father a child, because his wife was past child-bearing age. Some people had offered him money to leave his wife and enter into a sham marriage with a young South American woman who wanted to stay in Britain. But he was too much of a gentleman to enter into false wedlock with a Latin woman.

A gang of thieves operated in close proximity to the police station at Charing Cross. It was a fraternity of North African men, joined by one or two English comrades. They met in a very busy café in St Martin's Lane, and exchanged salaams with each other. Kasim despised this group when he overheard their conversations in Arabic while buying a coffee. Sometimes, he would spot one of the members of the gang accompanying a tourist on Charing Cross Road, whose pocket was going to be picked before the person had reached Cambridge Circus. It reminded me of the Thugs of eighteenth-century India, the worshippers of goddess Kali who attached themselves to the unsuspecting traveller, made friends with him, slipped a noose round his neck, and divided his money and baggage. In the evening, these men dispersed into many pubs around the West End where they ordered non-alcoholic drinks for themselves. They were devout enough to refrain from drinking alcohol, yet they had no qualms about lifting other people's belongings. Accountants who travelled with their laptops became squiffy after having a few drinks in a pub, and usually woke up to find their computers missing. One of the thieves dressed smartly like a door-to-door salesman and was always accompanied by an Englishwoman with a considerable bosom, who also wore a dark-coloured suit. The guise had made him a successful businessman. They went around shops and offices in the West End offering the laptops for sale. One of the Englishman in the gang, who found it difficult to remember the Arab names, called all his accomplices Abdul. The other one looked like an undercover detective to me. A trainee barrister, who was doing odd jobs in Charing Cross Road, helped these pickpockets with legal matters. They were also supported by many people working in Central London who would readily buy the stolen goods at give-away prices. Some of them haggled with the thieves over the prices. Once, a thief had cut his hand badly trying to remove an electronic tag from a pair of jeans in front of a prospective buyer, who offered him £5 for the item.

One afternoon I was surprised to find the kiosk shut – it was unusual to see it closed early. A few days later, when walking down Charing Cross Road again, I stopped for a chat with Kasim and mentioned that I had seen the kiosk closed a few days ago. He told me that he had received a telephone call from a police station in Brighton informing him that his thirteen-year-old son had been caught shoplifting in a toyshop. The police had tried to contact Pat but couldn't reach her. Kasim's worst fear had come true: his own son had committed an act for which he despised others. Kasim had closed the kiosk and driven to Brighton to pick up his son from the police station. His son had gone to Brighton for a day with his friends from the estate. The next week Kasim brought his son to the West End to buy toys for him. He was a sweet child, with the same curly hair as his father's. It was painful for Kasim to think that his son was living with his mother, who was an alcoholic. It also hurt Kasim to see his son growing up on an estate where it was very easy for him to pick up bad habits. He forgave him for the shoplifting incident and told him to ask his dad for money whenever he needed it. Kasim felt no kinship in London except with his son, and he was prepared to make sacrifices for his well-being. Kasim had learnt by living with Pat for a few years that the welfare state had corrupted her morally as well as others living on the estate. He didn't want his son to go the same way.

At the back of the kiosk there was a door leading to a small courtyard that Kasim had never opened since he had taken over the running of the kiosk. He used the space in front of the door for the storage of drinks. One day he opened the door in order to find the source of some dampness in the kiosk, and was surprised to see the courtyard littered with discarded wallets. The pickpockets had thrown these wallets in the courtyard after removing cash and credit cards from them, but left other things untouched. Kasim collected all the wallets to take them to Charing Cross police station. He had once himself been a victim of a pickpocket, but the thief had been kind enough to send him back his driving licence and other items by post. Unfamiliar with such places, when Kasim entered the Charing Cross police station, there was no one at the reception desk and he had to press a buzzer for attention. When an officer came out to the reception desk to assist him, Kasim handed him a bagful of wallets. The officer took personal details from Kasim. He wanted to know how long these wallets had been lying in his backyard. Then he asked Kasim whether he had a list of the items in the bag. He began to make a list in front of Kasim, and wrap each wallet in a plastic bag. The meeting lasted forty-five minutes. When Kasim was about to leave, he saw two backpackers entering the police station to report the theft of one of their wallets on Charing Cross Road.

A West Indian tramp always stood outside a cinema in cold and wet weather, asking passers-by for a cigarette. One evening, while taking a stroll along the west side of Charing Cross Road, I heard someone reclining in a doorway in the dark saying 'Alright Bhai' to me. When I stopped to find out where the voice was coming from, I saw someone lying on the floor in the dirt, a man with a white beard. It was the first time I had seen an Asian vagrant in the West End. I crossed over to the other side of the road near the Presbyterian Church to cut through Litchfield Street to reach Seven Dials. A Moroccan restaurant had laid out a carpet with floor-cushions on the pavement to create a souk in the cold climate, like a nomad who weaves a floral pattern on a rug to create a garden in his tent. At the corner of the road, a doorman guarded the entrance of a famous restaurant which served English food. Its exterior had a frosty look, suggesting that it was the haunt of people in need of privacy. A homeless person lay unconscious on the pavement, a few yards from the entrance of the restaurant, surrounded by empty cans of beer. A Black Cab pulled up in the narrow street, bringing diners to the restaurant. The doorman held the door of the cab open and an affluent couple alighted from the carriage to be ushered into the restaurant. When I reached Seven Dials, I found a group of young travellers resting around the central column. An elegantly dressed old woman asked me for directions to the Donmar Warehouse. The florists were carrying calla lilies and birds of paradise into a lock-up shop for the night. In the eighteenth century, the chroniclers of American history compared the tenements of New York to the Seven Dials and Whitechapel districts of London. Whitechapel had retained its character but Seven Dials had become fashionable.

A pot-bellied man, who usually sauntered along Charing Cross Road in the afternoon wearing medieval costume and carrying a staff in his hand, was talking to a street vendor. I had mistaken him for an out-of-work actor who must have played serious roles like King Lear. But when I heard his voice, it was very light and he sounded like a simpleton in his conversation, dispelling my assumption about his Thespian background. I also saw another person walking up and down Charing Cross Road regularly, dressed like a fisherman from Grimsby. Now I doubted his profession as well. It did not matter how bizarre a person looked in the West End: others took no notice of them. This was the theatre district, and the audience was used to the sight of costumes displayed in the windows of Angels & Bermans. Besides, there was always street theatre going on in the piazzas around here. It was natural to identify an eccentric with an artist. Theatre actors came to the West End on various pretexts. Some of them often visited the area for lessons at the Actors Centre in Tower Street. A few retired actors took long walks from Islington to have a vegetarian meal at a restaurant in Neal Street. The young and hopeful came here for auditions.

I found the kiosk shut for the whole week, and when I passed by again during the following week I asked Kasim's neighbour about his whereabouts. The neighbour informed me that the leaseholder of the kiosk decided to vacate the place one evening, and asked Kasim to fill black bin-liners with everything on the shelves. The leaseholder hadn't reached an agreement on the rent increase with his landlord, and had therefore decided to give up the kiosk after many months of wrangling. The kiosk remained closed for several months afterwards. No one wanted to pay the new rent demanded by the landlord, and Kasim had told me that it would be difficult for the landlord to find a new tenant. I wondered what happened to Kasim after the closure of the kiosk in Charing Cross Road. He was attached to the kiosk more than its owner, who had a few other businesses around this area. It was Gordon who told me after some time that Kasim was doing odd jobs in Edgware Road.

Post Office Counters Limited

The first place I stopped at in my new neighbourhood in North London was the post office. I wanted to enquire about the prices of postage stamps. The name 'post office' had romantic associations in my mind. It evoked the childhood memory of a colonial building on a riverbank in Srinagar where foreigners collected their letters at the poste restante counter. However, when I entered a London post office for the first time, I was surprised to see that it sold newspapers and magazines as well. There was an Asian man and a woman sitting behind a glass counter. The sub-postmistress looked angry. I asked how much it cost to send a letter within the country. She asked me if I wanted to send it first class or second class. I hadn't thought that the class system applied to the postal service too in Great Britain. The lady seemed too bothered to tell me the difference between the two.

I used my local post office often during the next two years to send my mail and to buy stationery. A trip to this post office gave me a glimpse of two worlds. It was the people of the neighbourhood who, as customers, offered apologies for the rudeness of the postmistress. Most people mistook the man behind the counter for her husband, but in fact he was her brother. She would become furious when customers referred to the man sitting beside her as her husband. At first I found this spectacle painful, but then gradually it became amusing. There was also a younger person working at the shop counter of this post office, whom I got to know after frequenting the shop for a few months. His name was Sanjay and he came from Mauritius. The postmistress and her brother, who owned the shop, were from Mombasa in Kenya. They belonged to a big Gujarati family who had come to Britain in 1968 and after a few years took over various small businesses in London. There were five brothers and four sisters in the family, and between them they owned a dozen businesses, including two post offices, three pharmacies and a few corner shops. All of their businesses actually constituted one joint business. Therefore, no member of the family ever borrowed money from a bank. They financed each other in acquiring new businesses.

Sanjay didn't know where his ancestors came from in India. He was lean, unlike the postmistress, who could pass through a door only with difficulty. He also had a good sense of humour. Sanjay was a post-graduate law student at the University of Westminster. As an overseas student, he was allowed to work only a certain number of hours. But the postmistress did not care about the law, as long as it benefited her financially. She did not pay Sanjay extra for working on bank holidays. Neither did he get any annual holiday while working there. She was not alone in exploiting an overseas student to her advantage. All the reputable businesses in London relied on the workforce of needy international students. Sanjay told me that it was impossible for him to pay for accommodation and his university fees if he worked only twenty hours a week. He was living in a bedsit in Berwick Street. The area was so fetid in the evenings because of the refuse lying around from the fruit and vegetable market that one had to hold one's nose to pass through it. But the guidebooks of London painted a romantic picture of Berwick Street, showing costermongers selling garlic and red chillies on the colourful barrows. Sanjay was embarrassed to tell anyone where exactly he lived.

The postmistress had carried colour prejudice with her from Mombasa to North London. She became alert every time a black person walked into the post office. That person would feel uneasy to see her thus alarmed. One day she was questioned by a black customer about her reaction. She replied that she was also an African, born in Mombasa. But this was not strictly true. She was loyal only to her own family. She mistreated Sanjay, who didn't speak Gujarati. He spoke French and English. The brother and sister swore at their customers in Gujarati. The postmistress was also well-versed in the use of argumentative phrases in English. 'Hold your horses, madam' she would exclaim in response to a complaint. Therefore, few people in the neighbourhood ever complained to her about the way she conducted her business. Many simply walked up the hill to another post office.

Sanjay said that the postmistress didn't like it that local people were waking up late, having breakfast in a café, and then coming to hassle her in the post office around midday, when she herself opened the shop at seven in the morning. She didn't trust her employee to have the shop keys, which meant that she worked twelve hours a day – seven days a week. However, she drove an expensive Mercedes convertible. I had once heard a car salesman at a showroom referring to the same type of vehicle as a Gujarati car. Some local residents were living in houses worth more than half a million pounds. But that didn't mean that they were not hard up for cash. In fact, the postmistress was very kind to one or two neighbours to whom she gave cash advances without interest against a postdated cheque – sometimes for amounts as little as £20. It is said that Gujarati businessmen started moneylending in Africa in the thirteenth century.

Some of the locals admired Gujarati folk for their business skills. Others were less impressed by their parsimony. The postmistress had instructed Sanjay to be an astute shop assistant. He was told not to offer carrier bags to customers as it cost the postmistress a penny each. He was also warned not to give a piece of sellotape to customers, or lend a stapler, so that they would buy these items from the shop. Sanjay risked his job if he didn't follow her orders. He was paid £120 a week for working forty hours in the shop. After a year, Sanjay asked his employer whether his wages could be increased to £125 a week. The answer he got was that he should cut down on his expenses rather than expect a rise. The postmistress said that her family of five could live on an outlay of £100 a week. But she didn't mention that they lived in a freehold house in North London, whereas Sanjay was living in a bedsit in a run-down part of town. The postmistress was shocked to see Sanjay entering a pub one evening. Not that she was horrified by the word 'alcohol', but she was shocked by the price of pub drinks. She ordered the toiletries for her family from a wholesaler, and her brother went to Vauxhall Bridge to buy fruit and vegetables in a big market.

The postmistress watched Sanjay on the closed-circuit TV in her back room. Sometimes, he would engage in small talk with a shy-looking woman at the shop counter. The next day the postmistress would say, 'I know you have been trying to chat up a woman in my shop'. The postmistress had remained single because she could not find a man to marry from her own caste in London. She and her brother considered their caste higher than other Gujaratis living in Britain. Being single meant that she lived a celibate life, unlike single people of the host society, for whom sex is usually central to their existence. The postmistress was flirtatious with a few of her customers, but it was only in jest. She was content with pinning up the pictures of one or two Bollywood stars on the walls of her back room. She also had pictures of her nephews and nieces hanging on the walls of her post office compartment.

It was exactly half past five in the afternoon when a woman with two babies in a pushchair reached the post office counter to cash her child benefit cheque. The postmistress was closing her counter, and the woman begged her not to send her away without cash, saying that she had no money to buy milk for her babies. But the postmistress, as usual, didn't budge. The sobbing woman asked the postmistress whether she had any children. But the postmistress was unresponsive. A bystander was so moved to see this heart-rending scene that he took a £10 note out of his wallet and offered it to the woman. The postmistress carried on with her chores.

If she had had children of her own , they would have been the same age as Sanjay. Sometimes a customer would refer to the postmistress, while talking to Sanjay, as 'your mother'. It would make him smile. The locals knew it for a fact that Gujarati folk employed only their own family members – even invalids – to run their business. On my visits to the post office, I would come across a frail Asian man carrying a big load of parcels from another Gujarati business for posting. I felt very sad to see that wretched man. The person who sent the invalid to the post office every day himself stood by the entrance of his shop like a sentry, huge and pot-bellied.

An American who lived in the neighbourhood was appalled by the insolence of the postmistress. Every time he asked for new-issue stamps, the postmistress sold him the old ones without telling him why. One day he said loudly, 'You guys shouldn't be running a post office'. There was also an Irishwoman in the queue, and the postmistress was being difficult with her because there was an accounting error in her passbook. The postmistress said that she was a qualified accountant, which the Irishwoman found hard to believe. 'If you were a qualified person', she said, 'you wouldn't be doing this job'. It was not often that the postmistress was challenged by a customer for her rudeness. English customers didn't utter a word to her, preferring to suffer in silence. They would apologize before saying, 'May I please have half a dozen postage stamps'. The only person who made the postmistress smile was a local tramp who came there every Friday to cash his dole voucher. He called her 'Miss World', and would sometimes compare her to Greta Garbo.

The sub-post offices in London offer a villagey type of service to their customers, closing for the lunch break in the afternoon. Office workers take a walk to the post office during their lunch break, only to find its counters closed. The sub-post office also remains open only for half a day on Thursdays. The office workers could not distinguish between a main post office and a sub-office. They also found it difficult to remember the capricious opening hours of their nearest post office. It gave the postmistress a chance to vent her anger. When a puzzled customer asked her the reason for the post office being shut in the afternoon, she would retort that the Royal Mail didn't pay her enough to keep the counters open throughout the day. Moreover, she was against the custom of selling postage stamps at the shop counter. There was no incentive for her in being philanthropic. It gave her pleasure to see others getting frustrated. She would go out of her way to order a magazine or a foreign language newspaper for a customer, but she never opened the door of her post office cabin on Thursday afternoons to get a book of postage stamps for an elderly customer. I often wondered if the closure of this branch would make any difference to the people of the neighbourhood.

Sanjay was accustomed to the incivility of the postmistress. He had found it very upsetting in the beginning but eventually learned how to grin and bear it. The customers could walk away from her, but Sanjay was not so fortunate. A friendly postman once jokingly told Sanjay that he was doing slave labour. But it rang painfully true to him. His employer distrusted people other than her own. One day, while picking a quarrel with a customer with whom she had been friendly before, the postmistress told Sanjay that you couldn't trust English people for a second. Sanjay knew well enough that she didn't trust Africans either. The postmistress herself worked fifty-two weeks a year behind the post office counter because she was mistrustful of others when it came to handling cash. She had employed one or two outsiders to work for her in the past, but they had to leave because she was suspicious about their trustworthiness. The postmistress had also employed a Gujarati woman whose husband had borrowed money from her. It was not clear whether the postmistress paid her wages or whether the woman was paying off her husband's debt.

One week I found a different woman working behind the counter. I assumed that the business had changed hands from one Gujarati family to another. Then I heard that the postmistress had gone on holiday for a week and a half, visiting relatives in Canada. It was her elder sister who was running the post office in her absence. The postmistress had also been to India for the first time ten years ago. She had been dismayed to see the shortage of toilet paper in such a vast country, and people using water instead. Since her family left Kenya, they had never returned to Mombasa. Her father had worked for the railways in Kenya, during the time of the Raj, travelling from Surat in Gujarat. In due course, he had set up his own business, which prospered, and he raised a big family in Africa. When he died, his children sold the business in Mombasa and moved to London. They were able to buy a small business in London, and added another five businesses to it in the next two decades. The postmistress was proud that she was running her own business in a middle-class neighbourhood of London.

She had taken on Sanjay as an apprentice who, in her opinion, would one day want to run his own post office, while she was herself looking for new business opportunities. It was hard work running a sub-post office in London. She had to balance the books once a week, sometimes staying in her cabin till late to accomplish this feat. But the books did not budge until she had filled her ashtray with cigarette butts. She was also unsure about the numerical skills of her brother who worked alongside her. Post Office Counters Limited (POCL) had finally decided to modernize its branches, and had recently introduced computers. It proved to be quite a challenge for the brother, who had told Sanjay a few months before that he held a degree in engineering. In fact, it took longer at first for the customers to be served after the introduction of computers. Post Office Counters Limited were handling more cash than many banks but they showed aversion to other methods of payment.

Once when I was travelling along a narrow Roman road in a tourist bus to the West Country, the guide claimed that people in Roman Britain attached their letters to a roadside post to be collected by a horseman, which was how the word 'post' came into use for sending a letter. It was the novelist Anthony Trollope (a post office employee) who introduced vermilion postboxes in Britain during Victorian times. The residents of my neighbourhood called them 'posting-boxes'. The Royal Mail was the first postal carrier in the world to establish a public overseas airmail service between London and Paris, in 1919. Two decades later, the Empire Airmail Scheme came into being to carry mail throughout the British Empire at a standard rate. The postmen in India wore khaki uniforms, unlike the 'robin postmen' in Britain, who wore red uniforms. One of the postmen I usually saw bicycling on the riverbank in Srinagar wore a khaki turban. I had mistaken him for a schoolmaster. But then I saw him entering the post office, of which the ground floor was used for posting letters and the first floor by postmen collecting their mail. The khaki turban worn by a postman was a mark of respectability.

Whenever an absent-minded person asked our postmistress a foolish question, she would burst out laughing. A man who looked like a habitual marijuana-user asked the postmistress if she sold 'a self-addressed envelope'. The postmistress replied that the Royal Mail had not yet got round to supplying its customers with such a thing. Another time, a well-known local poet, who was always lost in his own thoughts while strolling along the back streets, drifted into the post office to send a letter to America. The postmistress sold him one first-class stamp and a few more stamps to make up the right postage for a letter to America. It occurred to the poet to ask how they know the value of a first-class stamp in America. The postmistress grinned and told him that they don't have to know the value of our stamps in America. The poet was baffled by her reply. He also bought a few pens and some writing paper. She remarked that it should make him famous. The person standing in the queue behind the poet muttered that he was already famous.

Another time, the postmistress asked Sanjay to keep an eye on a vagrant who had just entered the shop. His breath and clothes smelled of alcohol. A Canadian woman in the shop recognized him as an actor who had played the role of an idiot-savant in many films.

The postmistress placed a small order for the supply of stationery with a sales rep who came by every Tuesday at nine in the morning. Since he was also a Gujarati, she spoke to him in Gujarati, interspersed with English words. Sanjay had taken the sales rep for a small-time businessman. Then one day, the postmistress sent Sanjay to the rep's warehouse on an errand. It was a very big warehouse, stacked to the ceiling with merchandise. Sanjay was intimidated by its size, yet only three or four men were working there. They were the brothers of the man, who came to take an order worth about £100 from the postmistress every week. He went around small businesses taking orders for the supply of stationery, while his brothers prepared the orders for dispatch in the warehouse. Even David Mamet, in his play *Glengarry Glen Ross,* expressed amazement at the way Gujaratis run their businesses.

One night thieves smashed a brick wall to break into the post office, using a sledgehammer. They got away with about £200 in small change. However, the noise didn't wake up the neighbours living in the flats above, people who usually made life difficult for the shopkeepers during the daytime by complaining about various noises. Among them was a stern lady who worked for the local council as a volunteer. The shopkeepers dreaded it whenever she came into their shops. The postmistress found it hard to believe that the neighbours had heard nothing while the robbers were carrying out their work. The next morning the Metropolitan Police sent a forensic team to take fingerprints, and the post office closed for the morning. Many customers expressed their sympathies to the postmistress. She became cheerful and friendly for some time after the break-in. It gave her a sense of distinction.

Sanjay established rapport with those who came into the shop often. But the postmistress extended her friendship to very few people. Among them were sales reps, for whom she was a valuable customer. She treated all other people, including a Law Lord who would come to the post office riding a bicycle, with disrespect. Another gentleman, wearing a suit and a bow-tie, introduced himself as a Queen's Counsel and asked the postmistress if she would witness his signature on a legal document. It made the postmistress feel important, so she obliged without hesitation. I always saw this person, wearing his dark suit and bow-tie, waiting for his washing at a launderette. Perhaps he was a retired Queen's Counsel and liked to be formally dressed even though no longer working. A senile couple used this post office often. The wife, who was writing her memoirs, was very frail, and she could walk only by holding the arm of her husband. I once saw the old man in the post office unaccompanied by his wife. When I asked after her, he said that she had lost her memory before finishing her memoir. Then there was the military historian who showed the postmistress a copy of the book he'd published about his experience in the war fifty years ago. He told her that it had been reviewed in the literary pages of a national newspaper just a week before. The postmistress told the military historian that she never had time to read a newspaper. It took her half an hour to bundle up the returns in the evening.

On Sundays, the postmistress's nephew and niece, whose pictures adorned the walls of her cabin, came in to give her a hand with the shop work. Both of them were at college during the week. Unlike their aunt, they were very pleasant and the shop became welcoming to its patrons on Sundays. The nephew and niece were also shocked by the rudeness of the postmistress towards others whenever she wanted to show who was in charge of the business. The postmistress had told Sanjay that the people of the neighbourhood were two-faced. They addressed her as madam inside the shop, but when they stepped out of the shop they called her a witch. She knew that all good manners were hypocrisy. Therefore, she had no time for the exchange of pleasantries with her customers. Even those people who occasionally borrowed money from her, and who therefore had reason to consider her kind-hearted, were upset by her rudeness. She was contemptuous of people who lived lavishly and sometimes needed to borrow £20 from her. However, many people forgave her in a condescending way.

These people also believed that Sanjay could bear his ordeal there because he had arrived in London not long ago, and was going through his rites of passage.

Sanjay was one of very few who, after going abroad, didn't send any money home. His parents owned a cottage in Port Louis, which they rented to holidaymakers. Because it was a small family, they could manage well with the income from their holiday business. Sanjay's parents hadn't been to college but it was their ambition to see their son obtain a university degree. They paid his fees for the first six months. During his induction at his new college, Sanjay's tutor, Mr Webster, told him that London was an international dustbin where you meet riff-raff from all over the world. Mr Webster himself was a devout Anglican. He always wore a blazer and also carried an umbrella. He said that he bought his clothes at a second-hand shop. Sanjay learnt a few weeks later that Mr Webster had married an international student from Peru a year earlier. He was a divorcee, who had lived on his own for ten years before he proposed to the student, who was enrolled at another college. The other teachers considered Mr Webster lucky to find happiness again.

Sanjay spent his first six months at the college in a distracted state. Then he took up a temporary job to pay an instalment of his college fees. He had been doing the same job for the last two years and spent more hours at work than at his studies. There were many international students at his college whose studies were taking twice the usual time. Some of them took their temporary jobs more seriously than their university degree. They drove second-hand cars and put on hair-cream to look affluent. It was enough for them to attend a college in London. Whether they passed or failed did not matter. Sanjay, on the other hand, wanted to finish his degree and return to Port Louis. He felt demoralized by working for the postmistress and had lost his self-esteem as a result of being shouted at so often in front of others.

One afternoon, while giving Sanjay a sharp rebuke, the postmistress said that a university degree didn't get one anywhere these days. Sanjay had made the mistake of giving a small piece of sellotape to a customer called Mrs Burke. The postmistress continued her lecture by asking why he wasn't trying to find a job elsewhere if he didn't like to work for her. Sanjay felt so deeply insulted this time that he decided to leave. The postmistress told him to come on Friday to collect his wages. When he went to see her at the weekend, she asked him to wait for her in the back room. She came in after a few minutes and lit a cigarette. The small room was quickly filled with cigarette fumes. She took her chequebook out of a safe and scribbled a cheque for £90. While passing him the cheque, she said, 'You don't have a job, and I don't have someone to work for me. Let us compromise.' But Sanjay thought that it was better to starve to death than to suffer at her hands again. He met Mrs Burke again a few weeks later in the high street. She didn't know why Sanjay had left his job and he was not going to tell her either. She asked him if he was managing all right and Sanjay was touched by her kindness. Mrs Burke had lost her own daughter in an accident a few months earlier, and had not yet overcome her grief. I met Sanjay again three months later in Central London. He had found a temporary job in a bookshop, had passed his university exams, and was looking forward to going home soon.

I stopped using the sub-post office after Sanjay left, preferring to walk uphill and use the main post office on the high street, whose staff were friendly and helpful. I asked myself why I had put up with the rudeness of the postmistress for all those months. The neighbourhood I was living in felt different, simply because I was using another post office. It was the letters I received from my friends in Kashmir that gave me consolation during those difficult days when I had failed to make a single friend in London. Sometimes, I would return home at midday to see if I had received a letter in the second post. I liked the idea of seeing a postman twice in a day. I occasionally saw a postman in my neighbourhood in Kashmir. But when he actually emptied a letterbox remained a mystery to me in my childhood. The letterboxes were painted in the same imperial red, and they looked similar to the cast-iron pillar-boxes bearing the insignia of the Royal Mail.

I visited the sub-post office again after several years. There was now a blonde girl working at the shop counter. Perhaps the postmistress treated her better than she had treated Sanjay. The postmistress looked older and tired. When I saw several people signing a petition at the post office counter, I asked the girl at the shop counter what it was about. She said that the Royal Mail wanted to close this branch in order to save money, and the people of the neighbourhood were signing a petition against its closure. They included people whom the postmistress had been rude to in the past, but they signed the petition out of solidarity and civility. I, too, signed the petition, now that I knew the reason for it.

The management of Post Office Counters Limited went ahead with their decision and closed this branch after four months. But they informed the residents of the neighbourhood about the option of using the main post office on the high street. Someone told me that the postmistress was not altogether regretful in the end to see the place close down. Her nephews and nieces didn't want to run a sub-post office. She couldn't find a buyer either for her business. After being made redundant by the Royal Mail the brother and sister decided to work in the pharmacy owned by their family.

London Taxis International

I was searching for a certain book in a bookshop on Fortis Green Road when my eye was caught by a picture of a cabbie on the jacket of a hardback. It was a memoir by a London taxi-driver. His face looked familiar to me. The next morning, in the taxi rank outside the hotel where I worked I saw a taxi advertising the book I had seen the day before, in big letters. The driver was leaning against his taxi smoking a pipe. It was his own memoir. After greeting him, I asked him about his book. He said that it was doing well. He had been on a few radio stations since the publication of the book two months ago and it had also been reviewed in the newspapers. 'The price of the book is £12.99,' he said, 'but I'm selling it to the boys for £10.' He always referred to other taxi drivers in the rank as boys. Most of them were over sixty years old.

A few days later, I walked into a dingy private cab office late at night in another neighbourhood to get a cab home. There were two Iranians manning the office. They told me that I'd have to wait fifteen minutes for the next cab. I was prepared to wait for half an hour and took a seat in the waiting area. There were a few notices on the opposite wall saying things like 'Drivers should pay their money upfront' and 'Drivers are not allowed to use the toilet'. One of the men asked me where I was from, thinking that I was also an Iranian. They spoke about the drivers of Black Cabs. The other man said they were all English and Jewish. The first part was right, but the second part seemed unlikely to me. My cab arrived after twenty minutes and I was happy to get out of the stale air of the waiting-room. Fabio, the cab driver, was a Brazilian who had taught history at schools in Sao Paulo before driving a cab in London. He was also a blues singer and a socialist. He asked me where I worked. I told him it was in a hotel. He passed me his business card and asked me to give him a call if a guest staying in the hotel wanted to order a private cab. Fabio mostly worked at night. The Black Cab driver had concluded his memoir with the seamy side of night work and the increase in the number of private cabs. The dust jacket of his memoir mentioned that the he was a member of a golf club in Hertfordshire.

Black Cab drivers were contemptuous of those who drove private cabs. The Black Cabs were driven by silver-haired Englishmen, whereas private cab drivers were all foreigners. Private cabs in London outnumbered Black Cabs by ten to one. The Black Cabs enjoyed all the privileges conferred upon them by law, while private cab drivers had a pariah status. The Black Cab drivers were praised for their 'Knowledge'. Yet, even though the hotel I worked for had changed its name more than ten years ago, Black Cab drivers persistently brought people to the wrong address, still associating this hotel with its previous name. Their 'Knowledge' was at least ten years out of date. Many of the drivers had passed their test forty years ago.

It was half-past-ten in the evening, and I was near High Holborn with someone who was picking up two or three friends from a hotel to take them to a South Indian restaurant in Panton Street, just behind the National Gallery. I would have liked to walk to the restaurant, but my host wanted to be there before last orders were taken so he hailed a Black Cab. We realized after ten minutes that the cab was going in the wrong direction, towards Islington. When we told the driver our destination again, he made a U-turn and followed the correct route to Panton Street, though we had to sit in the traffic for about twenty minutes. My host thought that the driver had seen us coming out of a hotel and therefore assumed we were new in town. He had been running a business in Central London for over twenty years and expressed his views loudly. The driver remained silent until we reached Panton Street. The cab meter registered a fare of £12. We gave him a £20 note. He drove off without giving us change. The waiters had already taken the last orders in the restaurant when we arrived, but the manager decided to keep the restaurant open later than usual and serve us food. He called a private cab for us at midnight to go back to High Holborn. It cost £6.

The taxi rank outside the hotel where I worked was empty one early evening when an elderly lady wanted a taxi. I walked up the road to flag a cab for her but there were none in sight. After a while, I spotted a cab with its orange light on; it stopped and I directed the driver towards the hotel to pick up the lady. When I got back to the hotel – a distance of fifty yards – the elderly lady was gone, whereupon the driver angrily demanded £5. I was not in the mood to get into an argument with him, so I paid him £5 for covering a distance of fifty yards.

It is quite common for Londoners to make a private cab wait for them but only very rich people can afford to keep a Black Cab waiting. It is not unusual either to take a private cab further than the destination for which the fare is paid. Fabio told me that his passengers paid him the fare to Finchley and then took him on to Southgate. The Black Cab author confessed in his memoir that the 'boys' did not pick up Irish people hailing cabs in the streets around the Kilburn area at night. A blonde woman and her fiancé had got into a Black Cab in Central London to come back to our hotel one night. The driver saw the couple fondling each other in the back of his cab. Thinking that the woman was taking a customer to the hotel in his cab, he pulled up and asked the couple to get out of his cab halfway from the hotel. They could not find another cab on the road and had to walk a long way to the hotel. I asked a regular Black Cab driver, who came to the taxi rank very early in the morning, about night work. He said that he didn't like to carry transvestites from Madame JoJo's home during the night and was happy to see private cab drivers doing the night work. Also, since the traffic was not bad during the night, it was unlikely that the meter would register a solid fare for a short distance.

The Black Cab Tours Service would find any kind of driver, even a Finnish-speaking driver, to show tourists around London. I once ordered a Black Cab for a group of Americans staying at the hotel to take them on a two-hour tour of London. The driver arrived on time. He introduced himself as Albert. It was a dull day, and Albert told the Americans that obviously they were here for culture rather than weather. It reminded me of a joke I heard on the radio many years ago. A writer from a Commonwealth country comes to London to receive a literary award. He takes a Black Cab from Heathrow to Central London. The cab driver, commenting on his nationality, says, 'Oh, so you're here to get a bit of culture then'. Black Cab drivers in London have a soft spot for Americans, who are more generous tippers than others. Perhaps this is because the drivers are the only Englishmen they can chat with in London. One of the drivers in the taxi rank wore a cowboy hat and a T-shirt with stars and stripes printed on it. When I first saw him, I thought he was an American cabbie. Then I saw him getting into an argument with a private cab driver, and I was baffled to hear his cockney accent. A group of four Americans got into the Black Cab only with difficulty. It had been designed to fit an Englishman wearing a top hat. But its width proved insufficient to accommodate four American tourists on one seat. So two of them sat on the folding seats opposite.

The Black Cab drivers threatened to boycott the hotel whenever they saw a private cab picking up someone from the lobby area. One of them would come to the desk to say that they would have us blacklisted. They deemed an inexpensive private car unsafe to carry a passenger. And when they saw an expensive car used as a private cab, they invoked the archaic licensing laws, their green badge and the Knowledge. The Black Cabs were also equipped with a ramp for wheelchairs. On one occasion I waited outside the hotel to help a guest in a wheelchair to get into a Black Cab. When it arrived, I asked the driver if he could open the ramp for the wheelchair. He tried to open it but the ramp didn't yield. The cab driver said that he had never used it. We had to carry the guest, along with his wheelchair into the cab.

Fabio was frightened to pick up anyone from a hotel which was picketed by Black Cabs. Their drivers had the privilege of using hotel facilities. Some of them brought their own tea from home in a Thermos flask and sipped a cup of it while polishing their cabs in the taxi rank. Others read tabloids while waiting for a fare, or idly smoked cigars and pipes.

Fabio came to the hotel now and again in the evening to pick up a fare when the Black Cabs were not around. He always struggled at the end of each month to pay for the insurance of his car. He was raising money to record his own blues album. He had lived rough for some time when he had moved from Sao Paulo to London four years earlier, sleeping in an attic on top of a cab office where he worked during the day. He didn't have many belongings: all he owned was a guitar and a few clothes, which he carried in a duffle bag. Fabio had played guitar on the streets in Central London before becoming a cabbie. He played the songs of John Lee Hooker and could attract a sizable audience. People enjoyed listening to his live music but they wouldn't buy it recorded on CDs. He felt embarrassed collecting money in his cowboy hat. So he gave up busking and joined a cab firm.

Fabio was asked to get a haircut when he joined the firm as a new driver. He showed me an earlier picture on the cover of a CD in which he had long hair tied with a bandana, observing that it would take him many years to grow his hair that long again. When he started out as a cab driver, he knew very few roads in London and relied on his passengers to show him the way. He learnt the routes very quickly. He mostly carried English people home late at night from bars and pubs around Charing Cross Road. They knew their way home, except when they were too drunk to wake up. He took such passengers to a police station as a last resort. Fabio also accepted fares to destinations where Black Cabs refused to go during the day, such as Tottenham and Millwall. He earned more than his fellow drivers, but he kept his passion for singing alive with whatever money he earned. He hired small venues to play guitar and sing the blues. In his car he carried leaflets advertising his gigs, to be distributed among people he knew. Sometimes, he passed a leaflet to a passenger as well. He made less money from the ticket sales than he spent hiring the venue. He gave tickets to other drivers for free. Only his close friends attended gigs. Others were too busy making money by working during the weekends.

The police stopped private cabs often during the night for various checks. I asked Fabio how the police were able to differentiate between a private cab driver and a normal motorist. Fabio said that private cabs were usually fitted with a two-way radio, and the police stopped a vehicle when they spotted an aerial on its boot. Sometimes they were joined by officers from the Immigration and Nationality Department. Although his mother was Brazilian, Fabio held an Italian passport because his father was Italian. He grew up in Sao Paulo speaking Portuguese and Spanish. He hadn't learnt Italian from his father. The police asked him a few more questions when they saw his proof of identity. Some of the private cab drivers spoke very little English and were frightened of being questioned by police on the road. If they were mugged by a passenger, they didn't report the incident to the police for fear of being questioned. They took precautions during the night by carrying only £10 or £15 in their pocket. They hid the rest of the money in their socks or under the driving seat.

Now and again during the night, a female passenger would become flirtatious with Fabio. He knew very well that the same woman wouldn't look at him when she was sober during the day. He found the women working in gentlemen's clubs more sincere than those working in offices. His fellow cabbies bragged about their night-time conquests. He was better looking than the average cab driver, but had failed to make such a conquest. However, he listened to the anecdotes of others with interest. He also knew that one or two of these knight errants claimed to have good fortune but spent all their earnings in a tart's boudoir. Having grown up in Brazil, he found the rigmarole of a relationship with a London girl very tedious. He could find consolation only in his music, which alone reflected and expressed his mood. He improvised these bitter-sweet songs on his guitar in solitude and gave his lyrics to an English teacher for corrections. His lyrics were better than his spoken English. The English teacher would change an article here, an adjective there. Fabio composed his songs in Spanish first and then translated them into English. The translation took longer than the original composition.

The private cab drivers guessed that Black Cab drivers earned over £70,000 a year. Black Cab drivers, for their part, believed that private cab drivers earned more money than them. The two nations of cab drivers were similar in one respect – both liked the cash-only policy. Black Cabs added 12.5 per cent surcharge on a credit card booking. Private cab operators rarely accepted payment by credit card. The rivals were unanimous in their dislike of those who didn't tip them. Both were reluctant to carry a black person as a passenger. It was not easy for a person to get back his or her property if left behind either in a private Cab or Black Cab. Anything left behind in a private cab might be returned to its owner immediately, or it might never be seen again. Whatever is left behind in a Black Cab takes a few days to reach their lost property office, which is open only until four in the afternoon from Monday to Friday. By the time a lost item reaches this office, its owner has most likely taken a flight out of Heathrow. The lost property office also charges a fee for the collection of the item.

Fabio said that Hackney Carriages – still in official use as a term for taxis – formed a powerful group. They could send a person to prison for using the word 'taxi' for a private cab. Hackney Carriages traced their clout to the days of the Civil War, three and a half centuries ago, when Oliver Cromwell granted them a monopoly to ply the streets of London for hire. This privilege has become a state of mind, in which only a Black Cab had right of way on the streets of London. They make a U-turn on the road anywhere they see someone waiting for a taxi on the other side of the road. A private cab driver would have his driving licence revoked for making such U-turns. They are courteous only to Americans visiting London. It gives them an opportunity to impart their 'knowledge' of London to visitors. They recommend

Rules – a restaurant in Maiden Lane where Charles Dickens used to have three-course meals – for dinner, and Scott's – patronized by Ian Fleming – for lunch. Other recommendations include Simpson's-in-the-Strand, and Browns for afternoon tea. They also highly recommend a certain pub for food and drinks. The Americans, who usually carry a copy of *London for Dummies* with them, find the recommendations of the Black Cab driver praiseworthy.

Fabio was interested in learning about the history of the Aztecs. He wanted to know how Hernan Cortez could conquer the Aztec capital with just two hundred men and horses. He had travelled from the New World to the Old in search of an answer. He went to various libraries in London during the day to consult books on history. The other drivers in the cab office raised their eyebrows when they learnt that Fabio went to a library. He never mentioned his pursuit again to anyone he worked with at the cab office. Fabio wanted to go to see the Aztec exhibition at the Royal Academy. I accompanied him there.

When we entered the first exhibition room, I heard the voice of an Englishman who was endowed with the gift of oratory. A crowd of well-groomed people, all with grey hair, had gathered around him. We were in time for a free lecture. When the crowd moved to the next room, I noticed a slightly-built man at their centre. He wore a badge labelled 'Curator', which explained his profound knowledge of the exhibits. His oratory brought to life the sedentary objects made out of stone. He made gestures only with one hand because his other hand was paralysed, his disability becoming invisible on account of his powerful voice, which filled the small gallery rooms. He apologized several times for the large exhibits being in such small spaces.

The Aztecs (which means 'men of the north' in Nahuatl) formed an empire in central Mexico for two hundred years until 1521, when a Spanish mercenary, Hernan Cortes, captured the last Aztec ruler. It is said that when Aztec culture flourished, it produced fine arts, poetry, philosophy and literature. But Aztecs did not have an alphabet. They used pictographs to write histories in codices and calendars on stone. The exhibition at the Royal Academy dealt mostly with the element of human sacrifice in Aztec culture. The Aztecs built temples in which they worshipped many gods, including Huitzilopchtli, to whom they sacrificed human beings by ripping out their hearts while they were still alive. The exhibition recreated the ritual of human sacrifice from altar to urns for feeding gods with the blood of mortals. It displayed cutlery used to rip open the ribcages of the warriors, and pots for the storage of flayed skin.

We followed the curator from one exhibition room to another as he invoked the names of Aztec gods to a bemused audience. It brought to my mind the scene at the Louvre described by Marcel Proust's mother: 'I see a group of English ladies and gentlemen emerging, following in the footsteps of a guide, who leads them at a furious pace, stunning them with the names of persons and gods of whom, as poor Louise used to say, "Old as I am, I can safely say that I have never heard of such a thing in all my life." Listening ecstatically, they kept running for fear of losing him. As they were leaving *salon carre* and entering *grande galerie*, the man negligently thrust out his middle finger behind him and said without turning round; "This is Charles I, by Van Dyck." Since the tone implied a minor work, they hardly looked. "Kings of England," they said. "Oh, we've got them at home." And they hurried on to catch the guide, who had already entered the next gallery.'

The curator thought it necessary to mention that the Spanish exaggerated the element of human sacrifice in Aztec civilization for their own ends. He mentioned the Inquisition and witch-hunts in Europe during that time, and the diseases spread by Europeans, though not deliberately, among the Aztecs. He also stated that the Aztecs knew about the wheel but didn't have animals big enough to pull it. That tells us how Hernan Cortez could conquer the Aztec capital with just two hundred men and horses. A new colonial city was built where the temples of the Aztecs stood before. It took a few hundred years for the population of Mexico City to reach 250,000 – the same figure pertaining at the time of the Spanish conquest, when the city was known as Tenochtitlan.

There were a few ornaments in gold on display. The conquistadores melted the Aztec ornaments into bars before offering them to their sovereign for his marking. Pointing to one such bar in a sealed showcase, the curator said that he believed there were similar bars in the gold reserves of the Bank of England. The last room was filled with images of Christianity propagated by conquistadores among the conquered souls. The history of Aztec civilization was written by conquistadores because the Aztecs did not have their own alphabet.

It had become dark by the time we came out of the exhibition halls into the courtyard. Water was gushing out, gently tinted by floor-lights, in the centre of the courtyard. The traffic was frantic. I caught the headline of an evening newspaper at a news-stand outside the Royal Academy. The paper declared that war had begun, with pictures of American bombers flying high in the skies. My heart became heavy. I wanted to go back to the Royal Academy to seek shelter among the Aztec gods. But the doors of the Royal Academy had been locked for the night. I walked with lagging feet towards the Underground. American tourists were coming out of Fortnum and Mason with bags full of souvenirs. The bookshop nearby, which supplies the royal household, displayed titles of light reading in its shop-window. The doorman of Le Meridien, who was wearing a Charles de Gaulle hat, held the door of a Black Cab open for an arriving guest.

I was puzzled when I saw a hazard warning light used for the first time on top of the signs for private cab offices in

Central London. A year later, it occurred to me that the reason for these orange lights fitted with revolving reflectors was to beckon people leaving pubs with blurred vision towards a cab office. Black Cab drivers interpreted the orange light differently – signifying a hazardous journey – but refused to work during the night. I had seen cylindrical lights with a revolving tube, painted in helical stripes, fitted outside barber-shops in London. These lights created an optical illusion when switched on. Someone had shown ingenuity by turning a hazard light into a sign for cabs. I noticed that some of the big hotels in London had the same flashing light affixed to their exteriors for flagging Black Cabs.

As for the name 'minicab', I found its use for private cabs in London ludicrous at first. Some of the private cabs were bigger than a Black Cab. To me, Black Cabs looked similar to a car made by Hindustan Motors. The sound of its engine, the screeching of its brakes, and its hubcaps reminded me of my own car in Kashmir. In fact, some of the small parts under the bonnet of an old Hindustan Motors car had 'Made in England' etched on them.

The Black Cab author painted a grim picture in his memoir of the future of Black Cabs in London. He prophesied that their right to ply for hire would eventually be challenged. Parliament had finally passed a bill, after many years of debating, to give licences to private cab operators in London. The drivers had to wait further to be licensed. But many private cab operators were sent temporary licences by the Public Carriage Office (PCO) in return for their application. They received another temporary licence when the first one became out of date, and the PCO simply carried on replacing one temporary licence with another. However, they were generally reluctant to issue licences to private cab operators. It was as if Parliament had legalized an immoral trade. The PCO constantly warned single women about the risk of being raped by a private cab driver in London during the night.

I knew Yousef through Kasim. He worked in a nearby cab office on Charing Cross Road. I usually saw him standing at the doorstep of his office late at night on weekends. He held a clipboard in his left hand, and controlled a crowd of people with his right hand, making them form a queue while they waited for the next cab to arrive. It gave him pleasure to make English people, who had ruled the world, stand in a queue and wait for his instructions. Twenty years ago, when he first arrived in England, he had found it upsetting to see English people walking the streets with downcast eyes. Yousef was born and brought up in Rawalpindi in Pakistan. He was well-built and wore a thick moustache, which made it easier for him to control the crowd. Now and again a plain-clothes cop would show him his badge in order to jump the queue and get the next cab as a privilege. Otherwise, he established firm law and order outside his office from midnight until the early hours of the morning. Yousef, who had lived in East London for many years, was eminently suitable for this job. The customers haggled over prices with him and he brought a market trader's skills to his part in the transaction, quoting his prices in 'ponies' and 'scores'. The drivers were very happy working with him. He also gave them directions for various destinations. Sometimes he made two passengers going in the same direction share a single cab for the benefit of both – the customers and the driver.

Yousef also gave directions to drivers from other cab offices who brought people into the West End. Unlike those who worked in other cab offices, who were often abusive, he was considerate with drivers. A few of them brought food for him from home. In winter, Yousef wore a long coat and gloves, and he kept himself warm by drinking cups of hot tea. Sometimes he sat on a footstool sipping tea with steam rising in the cold air. Now and again he would offer his footstool to a woman who found it punishing to keep standing on very high heels. The haggling over prices could easily turn into a brawl during the night. But Yousef always showed restraint with those who were in a mood to fight after being thrown out of a nightclub. The drivers refused to carry a massive women, who hurled abuse at them after emerging from a casino. Yousef always tried to find a driver for her who was not intimidated by her. She would create a scene if it took longer than usual for Yousef to find a brave soul obliging enough to drive her home. The bigger, stronger drivers drove off whenever they saw her. It was a frail driver who always took her home from the West End.

A female driver, perhaps the only female private cab driver working in the West End, worked for Yousef's cab company. Yousef was very respectful with her. He addressed her as 'madam' and she called him 'sir' in return. Yousef addressed all other women as 'my love' – East Ender style. A man standing in the queue told his wife, 'Look, he loves you', to cheer her up. Yousef was careful in allocating jobs to the lady driver, never sending her too far out of Central London.

Yousef called one of his drivers 'Chief'. He drove a white Mercedes with tiger-print upholstery. He had a fanciful sense of dress. One day I saw him with a group of people at an event. He wore traditional African costume, and the people who accompanied him addressed him as Chief. Perhaps it was his real title. I wondered if those people knew his night-time profession. When I exchanged greetings with him, he said that he had seen me somewhere before. I did not mention Yousef and the West End cab office and his safari car seats. He seemed so important to those who surrounded him that I thought it would dishonour him.

Yousef told me that most of the drivers who joined his cab office were looking for temporary work. A few went into other trades, but most of them drove a cab for many years. There was a high turnover of drivers in every cab office in the West End. Sometimes they drifted from one cab office to another. At other times they would leave the trade for a few months, and then come back after failing in another enterprise. I was puzzled by how many drivers waved to Yousef during the night. Then I came to know that all of them had worked with him previously. He let a few of them pick up a fare from his office for old time's sake.

It was a challenge for Yousef to ward off drivers known as 'pirates' in the trade from stealing his customers. A Rastafarian man once walked up to Yousef from across the road and said, 'Gentleman, can I borrow you for a price?' He belonged to the fraternity of pirates. But he did not transgress by encroaching on Yousef's territory. So Yousef was happy to do him a favour. It made the pirate credible as a legitimate driver in front of his customer.

Prices varied with the ebb and flow of the crowd in the West End. Yousef called the fluctuation in prices 'supply and demand'. In determining his price he took other factors into account, such as weather conditions and the time of the month. It was busier for him at the beginning of the month, when people had money to feed their cab habit, than at the end. It reminded me of Delhi, where the government banned the sale of alcohol at the beginning of the month, lest the poor spend their salary all at once. Sometimes, a customer would haggle with Yousef over a pound, but then give a generous tip to the driver.

The cab office belonged to the same person who owned the kiosk in Charing Cross Road. Yousef saw him only once a week in the early hours of the morning to hand over the cash to him. The number of drivers who worked for this cab office varied from week to week. They joined and then left the cab office of their own free will. The owner never wanted Yousef to say no to a new driver. The drivers found it hard when the office took on too many drivers but Yousef did not like to see the drivers who worked with him struggling for fares. He had himself worked as a private cab driver for some time. It was difficult for him to persuade the owner of the business not to take on more than a certain number of drivers, as it meant a decrease in the owner's earnings.

Yousef was concerned whether the Public Carriage Office would give the owner a licence to be a private cab operator in the future. He hadn't received even a temporary licence from the PCO. The office had functioned at its site for over twenty years. But Westminster Council would not grant it planning permission – a requirement in obtaining a licence from the PCO. Yousef said that he had been to the PCO in Penton Street in Islington a few times to obtain the necessary application forms to get a licence. Our erratic Black Cab driver had probably confused Panton Street in Piccadilly with Penton Street in Islington; I realized after many months that the Black Cab driver wasn't heading in the opposite direction purposely, even though Penton Street must have been well-known because of the PCO, whereas Panton Street might have seemed relatively obscure. Officials from the PCO had come to inspect other private cab offices in the neighbourhood. They wanted to know if the private cab operators who had applied for a licence kept a record at their offices of items left behind by passengers. They also wanted to know if those items were stored in a cupboard under lock and key. To record the loss of a mobile phone in a Black Cab, their lost property office would ask a caller for the sim-card number of their phone. Most people don't remember their phone number, let alone a sim-card number.

Yousef had a foreboding that Westminster Council would not grant planning permission to the owner of the business, and he would lose his job. I asked him what he would do in that case. He said that he would go back to driving a cab for a living. But it would be a great come-down, since it gave him a sense of authority being in charge of a number of drivers. Nonetheless, he felt that he would be better off financially by driving a cab. It didn't matter so much for the owner, who had other businesses besides the cab company. Yousef was trying very hard to persuade Westminster Council to grant the operator of the cab office planning permission. But he felt that he was fighting a losing battle.

At the end of my first year in London, I decided to take a short ride in a Black Cab in Central London just for the experience. I hailed a cab on the Strand to go to Wigmore Street. The driver, who was about seventy years old, was an amiable character. He was driving a new cab made by London Taxis International. I did not like the look of the taxis made by Metrocabs. The rumour that Black Cab drivers earned £70,000 a year came to mind. If it was true, it was unlikely that I would find a seventy-year-old man still driving a cab on the road. While chatting with this elderly cab driver, I asked him an absurd question: How much would it cost to take a Black Cab to York? 'Oh Blimey!' he replied. 'It would cost you a few hundred quid. Six hundred quid or more, I can't tell you exactly.' Perhaps, he had never accepted a fare outside Greater London.

Mariam in Marylebone

Mariam was twenty-one years old when she moved to London from Tehran. Someone told her that it was already too late for her to be integrated into a new society. Mariam loathed that person for her premonition. She had travelled to London with her brother, who was a few years younger than her. They lived in the same flat for the first five years. Then her brother got married and Mariam moved out of the flat. She found a place in Marylebone, where she has been living for the past ten years. Mariam's father had been killed in the aftermath of the revolution in Iran, and her mother lived with her elder brother in Tehran until her death a few years earlier.

I met Mariam through Abbas, whose wife Shireen was a friend of hers. It was on a special night, the time of year when Iranians remember their dead: not only those who died in the long war with Iraq but also anyone who has passed away in the last few years. Mariam hadn't assuaged her grief at the death of her mother. She wanted to go to the Imambara (a building maintained by Shia Muslims for the purpose of celebrating Moharram) in Stanmore for the remembrance of her mother. The Iranians keep vigil during this night and illuminate cemeteries with candles. The night is also marked as a celebration of the birth of Imam Mehdi – the twelfth Imam of Shia Muslims. In the royal stables of Isfahan, in olden days, two horses were always kept saddled, one for the second coming of Mehdi himself, the other for his lieutenant, Jesus the son of Mary.

After moving to London Mariam wanted to become a nurse, as she had been inspired by the life of Florence Nightingale, who tended patients in hospitals during the Crimean War. But she had to learn a new language before applying for admission to a nursing college. She spent her afternoons in a local library reading english language textbooks or sometimes trying to make sense of newspaper headlines. In the mornings, she attended classes in a college to learn English. It was hard to make friends with fellow students at the college because they all spoke different languages. So Mariam had to be content with the company of her brother. They passed all their time together. A few years later, Mariam's brother fell in love with a Macedonian woman, whom he married after a few months. Consequently, Mariam had lived on her own for the last ten years. It would have broken her mother's heart if she were alive.

Shireen had tried very hard for many years, without success, to find someone for Mariam. Shireen, who was much younger than Mariam, was herself born in London of Iranian parents. She gave them a hand now and again working as a waitress in the café they owned in Marylebone High Street. Shireen studied medicine at University College London. Mariam worked as a nurse in Middlesex Hospital in Mortimer Street. Uninitiated in the art of seduction, she had resigned herself to her fate after failing to find a man.

Abbas and Shireen were sympathetic to Mariam. They understood her suffering because of the trials of their own parents, who had spent their childhood in Iran. It had taken them a lifetime to come to terms with their loss. Abbas' own father was an Iranian who had fled the country during the time of revolution. He had married an Anglo-Indian woman in London. Abbas was fair-complexioned, but he looked very much like his father. Abbas' father belonged to a group of Iranian émigrés in London who had been meeting once a week in the tea-room of a hotel for the last twenty-five years, waiting for the revolution to be rescinded so that they could go back to their homeland. These weekly tea-room meetings had become more informal occasions for the aging émigrés who yearned to return to Tehran one day. Sometimes, they exchanged old photographs from the time before the revolution. Those who attended the tea-room meetings were all men, but they were occasionally joined by a cheerful-looking woman. When she presided over the meetings, all the men listened to her attentively. Among the usual participants was a man who wore his hair long and spoke very little. He was a poet, who translated the sorrows of émigré life into verse, which he distributed among his fellow émigrés now and again. The children of these émigrés, who knew only the country of their birth, could not relate to this group of exiles. A few of them had married women from other countries. Others had remained single.

Abbas and Shireen had met at medical school. Abbas, who was three years older than Shireen, had qualified as a doctor a year before we met. Shireen had two more years to go before she could become a doctor. She had married Abbas six months ago. Shireen's mother wanted her to marry a cousin, but Shireen was in love with Abbas. As she could not leave home and live with Abbas before she married him, the couple decided to have a small wedding ceremony. They went to the town hall on Marylebone Road for the registration, and then proceeded to an Iranian restaurant for a banquet, organized by Abbas' mother. She was a gracious hostess at the banquet. Live Iranian music was played in the restaurant. Shireen's parents had also attended the wedding, having finally accepted Abbas as their son-in-law. It was an emotional occasion for them because Shireen was their only child. In truth, they would have liked the wedding to be on a grander scale.

Mariam considered Shireen lucky to have found Abbas at the right time. Mariam herself was not so fortunate. There were very few male nurses working for the National Health Service, so her chances of finding a man at work were minimal. Many people believed that nurses were always looking for an opportunity to pounce upon a doctor, and were readily available to anyone, including the patients they tended. But Mariam was brought up in a society where men paid a 'bride-price' for the guaranteed chastity of a woman, and she was unwilling to live with a man who might one day ask her to marry him. It was customary in Tehran for a man to wed a woman first and then share a bed with her. Mariam was plump, unlike Shireen who was very slender, and didn't attract the attention of many men – only those she found loathsome. Some years ago, her friends persuaded her to make an effort and she put a personal ad in the classified section of an evening newspaper. She agreed to meet one of the men who responded to her advert. It turned out badly and put Mariam off such enterprises forever.

I was uncertain in the beginning about how to pronounce the place-name Marylebone. I heard some people pronounce it as Mary-le-bone; others preferred to call it Marl-e-bone. I faltered at the many variations of this street-name. Some years later, an American asked me how people in London pronounced the name, reminding me of my confusion during my first few months in London. I also knew the parish of St Mary-by-the-Bourne along the Ring Road. Then one day I took a road from Wigmore Street to reach the outer circle of Regent's Park, and found the narrow Marylebone Lane widening into Marylebone High Street. There were a few boulangeries and patisseries along this High Street. The neighbourhood seemed affluent. The Oxfam shop was so well-stocked with books that it looked like a bookshop. The High Street appeared far-removed from the hustle and bustle of nearby Oxford Street. The American International University was situated in the middle of a row of shops. It had decorative textiles hanging in its glass-front, in contrast to the office of the American World University, which I had seen above the shops in Brick Lane.

I visited Marylebone High Street again a year later to meet Abbas and Shireen in a coffee shop located at the ground level of a modern block of flats. The coffee shop was part of a chain started less than ten years earlier by an Iranian brother and sister who had become a legend in the business world. Shireen's parents owned a small café at the other end of the street. The coffee shop had a relaxed atmosphere compared to the boulangeries and patisseries further along the road. When I passed through the street for the first time, I had doubted that those French cake-shops would serve me coffee without me ordering something else with it. The coffee shop was a precursor of Starbucks, the American coffee shop chain which appeared in London five years later.

Shireen told me that her parents had been working in their small café for the last twenty years. She guessed that the secret of success in the business world was to make others work for you. Her parents had arrived in London without any capital. The people who left Iran after the revolution were either those who had money and were threatened by the aftermath of the revolution, or those who opposed the revolution on ideological grounds. Shireen's parents belonged to the latter group. It was an arduous task raising capital to open a small café in Marylebone High Street, especially as they had no recourse to bank loans. They had worn themselves out working three hundred and sixty-four days a year. Shireen wanted them to sell the café now and retire. However, she was not sure how they would fill their days if they weren't serving others tea and coffee. Their work was their only consolation while living as exiles in London. It made their wretched existence bearable. They had waited for more than twenty years for the rule of clergy in Iran to end so that they could return home. With the passing of each year, that seemed more and more improbable.

Mariam lived in a studio flat in a block of flats above the coffee shop. She often went to see Shireen's parents in their café. They treated her like their own daughter, because they understood the sadness of living alone in a flat in Marylebone. They also invited her to their home every year to celebrate the Iranian New Year on the twenty-first of March. Shireen's parents became anxious if they didn't see Mariam for a few weeks. They had once sent Shireen to knock at the door of Mariam's flat when they hadn't seen her for a month.

Mariam had failed to make friends with anyone else in the neighbourhood after living in Marylebone High Street for ten years. She found it oppressive to see beautiful couples thronging the patisseries in the neighbourhood. It made her conscious of her own isolation. It also reminded her of the words of the sibyl who had foreseen her wretchedness. Mariam went to Baker Street to buy her groceries, avoiding delicatessens in Marylebone High Street. Their customers were slim and elegant ladies who sought longevity by eating exotic health foods. Mariam had no such desire to live a long life. Baker Street offered Mariam a retreat from the cosiness of Marylebone High Street. Baker Street, the starting point of the tourist trail in London, was where the visitors boarded the sightseeing buses. The bustle around the intersection where Baker Street cut through Marylebone Road made Mariam forget her loneliness. She usually sat in a shabby corner café, watching people pass by and women buying glossy magazines at a news-stand on the pavement. The cover stories of these magazines were more or less similar: lots of articles about how to improve one's sex life. Mariam herself never bought a glossy magazine. She was unfamiliar with the life which the magazine instructed its readers how to improve. Mariam mostly read romantic novels for women, and these novels had falsified her sense of reality.

I had heard the name 'MCC' in Kashmir during my adolescent years, without knowing that it was a cricket ground in Marylebone which gave the club its name. There were a few clubs of the same abbreviation in various neighbourhoods of Srinagar, the names of which began with the letter M. These clubs advertised on the hand-painted signboards which hung outside their makeshift offices, showing men in white uniforms playing cricket. As a child, I was fascinated by the art of the person who painted these signboards. Sometimes, I watched him at work outside his workshop by the roadside where he displayed his signs. The figures on the signboards took form over several days. He painted the head on one day, then the body on the next day, and the background landscape on the day after. He displayed the finished signboard outside his workshop for a few weeks before it was delivered to a customer. The workshop contained a myriad of small paintboxes and paintbrushes in various sizes. The floor was splashed with various coloured enamels as if it had been painted by Jackson Pollock.

I had taken a wrong turn out of Regent's Park and circled a roundabout a few times. A tall building by the roundabout housed a hotel. On the other side of the roundabout, I saw stands for spectators rising above a wall in what appeared to be a sports ground. I passed the same ground again a few months later and came to know that it belonged to Marylebone Cricket Club. The club was in the news for not letting women become members. Because of the club's exclusive male status lottery funding was withheld. I met the England Cricket team a few years after the MCC had agreed to allow women to become members. The team was playing a test match at Lord's and the hotel I worked at was hosting the team for one week. The night before the match began, the players arrived by coach at the hotel, wearing blazers and beige trousers. A few minutes before their arrival, Robert, the concierge, told me that he was expecting a group of supercilious men. He was familiar with the cricket team as they had stayed at the same hotel six months ago. When Robert held the door of the hotel open for them, they walked past him without acknowledging his presence. An Arab guest, who held court in the lounge, shouted a salaam at the captain of the team. The captain was disconcerted by the greeting from an Arab, glanced briefly at him, then walked on by, ignoring the greeting. There was also a white-bearded man with a rosary in his right hand waiting in the lounge. He got up and stopped one or two cricketers in the corridor, shook hands with them, and spoke to them for a few minutes while holding their hands before he took his seat again in the lounge. Having noticed me watching the cricketers hesitantly shaking hands with him, he called me over and gave me a visiting card with his name and a few international phone numbers printed on it. He told me that he was hired by the Metropolitan Police to protect the cricket team, and showed me his shirt, which had MCC embroidered on it. I would almost have believed him, had I not asked one of the cricketers if he knew the man. I was informed that the man was one of their most ardent fans and followed them everywhere. But he was quite harmless.

In the evening, the cricketers wanted to go to the Criterion Brasserie for dinner so they asked Robert to arrange a coach for them to take the team to Piccadilly. The wives and girlfriends of the cricketers left a bit earlier and went elsewhere for dinner. The next morning, the team came downstairs to the hotel restaurant to have their breakfast. The captain sat aloof in one corner of the restaurant as he didn't like to socialize with his team. I began to understand the meaning of the word 'supercilious', which Robert had used to describe the team. All the cricketers had ordered a copy of the same newspaper to be delivered to their rooms in the morning. It was a feature of their conservatism that they didn't want to be exposed to differences of opinion in the more liberal newspapers. On the fifth day of the Test the English cricket team lost the match. This time, it was against the Sri Lankan team. In fact, they had been losing matches for some time. When the team came back to the hotel in the evening, the players looked humiliated. But the other residents in the hotel hardly took any notice of them. The imperial game of cricket had lost its importance and other sports were now preferred. The cricketers didn't want to stay another night at the hotel so they packed their bags and left for the Home Counties.

I went to meet Abbas and Shireen again a few months later in the dingy café near Baker Street where Mariam spent her idle hours. It took me a little while to cross over to the other side of Marylebone Road on my way to the café. As I came out of the tube station, I had an encounter with Sherlock Holmes cast in brass. A group of students were loitering outside their college. I waited for half an hour in the café for others to arrive. As I sat there, I watched a great number of people walking up and down Baker Street. The world appeared to me in a state of flux and it dawned upon me why Mariam preferred Baker Street to the comparatively quaint Marylebone High Street. It was an ideal place to seek solitude, and the time seemed to pass very quickly.

Abbas had organized a picnic in the park for a few people. Its purpose was to provide an opportunity for Mariam to meet a widower called Hassan, a friend of Abbas' father, who was keen to marry for the second time. It was an oriental-style matchmaking. Abbas arrived with Hassan, and a few moments later Mariam and Shireen showed up. We all took a walk towards Regent's Park, passing the patina-coloured dome of the planetarium before we reached York Gate, leading to the outer circle of the park. The cream-coloured villas were intruded upon by a modern-looking concrete building. I had always wondered about the people who occupied that building. I noticed a name-plate near its entrance: 'The Royal College of Physicians'. A lady wearing a sari emerged from the building. The lawns in front of the terraces had been mown by gardeners, giving the air a smell of freshly cut grass. The lawns were enclosed by an elegant wrought-iron fence. As we took our leisurely walk on the circular road, the master-plan of John Nash unfolded before our eyes. One of the terraces, built in Bath stone, had polished doors made of oak. It was followed by the long façade of a stuccoed terrace with a pediment of statues. A small sign at the entrance of each terrace indicated that it was part of 'Crown Estate'.

A cobbled street between two terraces was being filmed by a crew of cameramen. They were recreating a Victorian street scene. A pair of Hansom cabs were drawn by well-groomed horses from the nearby barracks. The cabmen wore hats and gloves. We took a road leading to the Inner Circle of the park. A few joggers wearing headphones walked past us very briskly. Shireen chose a spot by a rose garden for all of us to sit down and spread out a blanket on the grass. She had also brought some snacks and savouries. It was a dull day, the sun hidden behind the clouds. Mariam, who had never met Hassan before, cast furtive glances at him. But she didn't speak to him in front of the others. Perhaps she knew that they were going to be left alone in due course. And sure enough, Abbas and Shireen announced that they wanted to go for a stroll around the park. I volunteered to join them. We walked towards the other side of the park. An armed policeman stood outside a villa in the park holding a gun close to his chest. I could see from a certain distance that an American flag was flying at an acute angle on top of the entrance of the villa. When Abbas and Shireen returned to join Mariam and Hassan, I made my way back towards Baker Street.

I was curious to know if Abbas and Shireen had succeeded in their matchmaking venture. I had doubts about it. Mariam had looked uneasy in the park, and Hassan didn't look very happy after seeing Mariam. When I met Abbas and Shireen again a few weeks later, I asked them about the outcome of the rendezvous. It turned out that Mariam had disapproved of Hassan, who had asked her how much money she earned per hour in her job as a nurse. He had heard from someone that nurses could earn as much as £18 per hour. Hassan himself worked as a cashier in a Bureau de Change, where he was paid £6 an hour and it had startled him to learn that Mariam was paid three times as much. Hassan was fifty years old, already thinking about the meagre pension he could get after his retirement. Mariam felt that Hassan was more concerned about his finances than finding a wife. Abbas and Shireen had more sympathy with Mariam than with Hassan. Abbas said that Mariam had found herself living in a society in which a sexual relationship was central to people's existence. Anyone who did not participate in this ritual was deemed to be a pariah. Shireen said that Mariam, who had become self-conscious over the years, was standoffish in her relations with other women at work, in case her fellow workers misunderstood her sexual orientation. A few years ago, Mariam had developed a close friendship with another nurse at the hospital. Then she had heard people talking about their friendship behind her back. Mariam was therefore glad that a hospital porter had fallen in love with her friend, and she saw very little of her afterwards.

Abbas went to the Imam-bara once a year on the eve of the tenth of Moharram. He usually visited the Imam-bara in Kilburn where Iranians living in London gathered for mourning. Mariam went to the Imam-bara in Stanmore where Gujarati Shias assembled during the first ten days of Moharram every year, as she didn't like to meet the sort of Iranian women who had dyed their hair blonde but covered their heads with a black chador, as they did in Kilburn. Abbas and Shireen wanted to accompany Mariam to the Imam-bara in Stanmore because her mother had died during the last year. I asked Abbas if I could go to see an Imam-bara with him on the ninth of Moharram. He didn't mind being my guide and we agreed to go there by tube, Stanmore being the final stop on the Jubilee line. Shireen drove Mariam there in her car to Stanmore.

When we came out of the tube station, we walked along London Road and turned off into Dennis Lane at an intersection. A few blocks of flats gave way to detached houses, camouflaged by pines and other trees. It felt like a walk through rural woodland. The neighbourhood looked prosperous. A 'Wild fowl' sign could be seen on the land. Many cars were going up the hilly road, driven by grim-faced Gujarati Khojas. Several were driven by women whose heads were covered in black chadors, and they carried only women passengers. There were no pedestrians on this road. We passed a fine hall on the way, the interior of which, I learned later, was decorated by William Morris and Burne-Jones.

The road joined Wood Lane as a T-junction. There were volunteers outside the Imam-bara directing cars to a parking lot. Formerly known as Warren House, this old Georgian house had only recently been converted into an

Imam-bara. It had once belonged to Sir Robert Smirke, the architect of the British Museum. Men and children were standing in the forecourt of the house. Many of these children, wearing black trousers and black shirts, looked plump. A few children were pouring drinks of vanilla-flavoured milk into plastic cups for newcomers. The women disappeared into a separate part of the Imam-bara.

When Khojas bought Warren House in 1987, there were about a thousand families of their community resident in London. It was a prosperous community, mostly living in North London. They had spent a few million pounds on the refurbishment of Warren House, and they had also acquired more land around the Imam-bara since then. Gujarati Khojas had a lot in common with 'Banias' – the Hindu traders who are known for their trading skills. The Khojas had settled in many African countries during the time of the Raj. They had built Imam-baras in Dar-es-Salaam and Zanzibar and had moved to London when the East African countries gained independence. I recognized a few businessmen who traded in North London in the crowd.

We waited in the forecourt until everyone went inside the hall. There was also a marquee pitched in the grounds. The hall was packed with men and children. I sat near the entrance of the hall to have access to fresh air. Volunteers closed the doors and switched the ceiling fans on. It was winter and the air outside was crisp. Another volunteer switched on a free-standing microphone near the front row.

A Khoja stood up and read elegiac verse from an old piece of paper. It took me a few minutes to understand that the verse was written in Urdu. But the Khoja's Urdu was unintelligible. I was waiting for a Zakir – Shia mourner – to appear. But I saw a Molvi – a cleric – instead. He had been flown in from Karachi by the Khojas to narrate the events of Moharram in AD 680 to mourners at the Imam-bara for the first ten days of the month. The Molvi had a melancholy face and wore a karakul and a long collarless black coat. He climbed up to a raised platform seat to deliver his discourse. He began with the events of the first day of Moharram in the year 61 AH at Kerbala. There was so much passion and vigour in his voice that I was myself moved by his power of narration. I could hear sobbing coming from the audience. A closed-circuit TV camera was focused on the raised platform. Perhaps it relayed the Molvi's speech to women sitting in the separate part of the Imam-bara. The Molvi mentioned the second coming of Imam Mehdi and his lieutenant Jesus Christ. Then he condemned gluttony and lechery in modern times.

The Molvi was gradually bringing his performance to its finale. Mention of the names of women and children caught in the events of the tenth of Moharram at Kerbala worked up the men in the audience. Their crying became louder and louder. The noise was picked up by the microphone and was amplified by speakers in the hall. When the noise reached a certain decibel-level, the microphone cut off automatically. People in the congregation were responding to the passion in the Molvi's voice more than they followed his words. The lights in the hall dimmed and everyone stood up. The men standing in the middle of the hall formed a circle and started beating their chests. A few took off their shirts to flagellate their torsos. It took practice to beat chests in a synchronized manner, like the beating of African drums. The hall of the old Georgian house resounded with the beating of ribcages. A wooden cot draped with multi-coloured fabrics was passed over the heads of the men who filled the hall. The crowd raised their hands to touch the cot in order to receive the blessings of twelve Imams.

We decided to leave the Imam-bara a few minutes before the end of the ceremony. The children outside the hall were serving hot tea and I saw a notice for the Sunday school at the entrance of the Imam-bara. We took the same route back to the tube station. The road was quiet; there were no longer cars going up and down as their drivers were still inside the Imam-bara. Abbas said that he went to an Imam-bara once or twice in Moharram every year because he had grown up listening to the events of Kerbala from his father. These events had become a part of his existence. In fact, his father had named him 'Abbas' after one of the Kerbala martyrs. I asked Abbas what he made of Molvi's pronouncements on gluttony and lechery. He replied that those were sins of the flesh, according to Christopher Marlowe, and a man can commit worse sins. Abbas told me that the Khojas had shown restraint in their expression of grief at the Stanmore Imam-bara, compared to those who gathered at the Imam-bara in Kilburn, where flagellation entailed shedding of blood. It was customary in many parts of the world that a prosperous community showed restraint, while the poor shed their own blood.

Many people in Iran, including Abbas' father, had believed that the clergy would return to Qum and Mashad after the overthrow of the Shah. But they had not expected them to stay in power for a quarter of a century. When Bani-Sadr was dismissed from office in 1981, it was a great blow for Abbas' father, who wished to return to Iran. His memories of the aftermath of the revolution were very painful. He had lost many friends whose funerals he could not attend because he was living in exile. Moharram was the month of the year that enabled him to grieve over the loss of his friends and his homeland. The congregation at an Imam-bara during Moharram was known as 'Majlis' – the same name as the Iranian parliament. Abbas, closer to his father than his mother, shared the grief of his father by attending the Majlis. His Anglo-Indian mother had taught him Marlowe's *Doctor Faustus* when he was young. Because he had an understanding of both eastern and western traditions, he didn't condemn one culture in support of the other, like many of those who are caught between them. Abbas was liked by those who worked with him at the hospital. Mariam was also very fond of him. He always wanted Shireen to take good care of Mariam as he understood her situation more than anyone else.

Shireen's parents were celebrating the Naurose – New Year's Day – with a feast. Abbas and Shireen invited me to join them on this occasion. I couldn't say no, since Abbas had obliged me by taking me with him to the Imam-bara. Shireen's parents had invited a few other people to celebrate the Naurose at their home. It was a small house with a living-room and kitchen on the ground floor, and a bedroom and bathroom upstairs. I was expecting a fine Persian rug in the living room. I found an Afghan Kilim instead. A few black and white photographs of Shireen's grandparents, taken in Iran before the revolution, were hanging on one wall of the living room. There were also a few pictures of Shireen as a little girl on another wall.

Shireen's father, a courteous person, came into the living room to shake hands with me and welcome his guests. Shireen's mother was busy in the kitchen, from which there came a smell of braised meat. Mariam was helping Shireen's mother with the preparation of Chalo Kebabs and other Iranian dishes. Shireen's father passed round a selection of dried fruit to his guests, among them a Peruvian couple who worked for Shireen's parents in their café. It was an elaborate feast. The starters were served with flat bread. The main courses came with trimmings, and there was baklava for dessert. Shireen's parents were professional caterers who served food to scores of people in their café every day. They treated Mariam with affection. Perhaps their café was her only consolation while living in Marylebone High Street.

Now in her mid-thirties, she had given up hope of finding someone to marry and preferred to get on with other things in life. Hassan was the last man she had agreed to meet, over six months ago. Abbas and Shireen thought that it was not sensible to persuade Mariam to find an older man for herself. She looked happier now that she had stopped worrying about getting married.

Bloomsbury Blues

An Englishman who lived in my area told me that he was moving to Bloomsbury. I had traversed his new neighbourhood many times by bus without knowing that it was called Bloomsbury. Then one day, while travelling on the upper deck of a bus, I noticed Gower Street becoming Bloomsbury Street at the lower end of the road. Whenever I passed through this area it gave me a feeling that London was made of bricks. While going up Woburn Place I saw a big building with semicircular brick columns in its façade. There was also a very big hotel made of bricks along this road. I saw one shuttle-bus going in and another coming out of the courtyard of the hotel. The bar in the hotel was called 'London Pub' and it sported the mock façade of a Victorian pub. There were one or two car rental company offices along this road. Another hotel further down the road housed a casino. I liked the Gower Street part of my bus journey. The buildings on one side of the road were made of bricks, and those on the other side were made of Portland stone. The brick buildings were covered in black soot and had been turned into small hotels. The buildings made of Portland stone belonged to University College London. The brick houses opened into a square where Gower Street met Bloomsbury Street. The houses around the square had chandeliers fitted on their upper floors, which appeared to be switched on even in daylight.

In the University area was an ornate corner building occupied by a bookshop. For many years, I was curious about what it was like inside. Then one evening, I got off halfway through Gower Street on my bus journey home from work and went in.

The bookshop had a broad wooden staircase leading upwards to the first floor and downwards to the basement. The alcoves on the staircase landings featured busts of Hippocrates and Socrates. The staircase became very narrow at the upper floors. The bookshop was very busy. It was the beginning of the academic year, when commercial banks gave free book vouchers to freshers as a reward for opening an account with them. Some of the students looked shocked by the prices of their purchases. Evidently I was visiting the bookshop at the wrong time of year as it was too crowded for me to roam around, so I decided to leave without browsing.

I returned to the bookshop a few weeks later. The students were having their mid-term break, and the bookshop was very quiet. Shop assistants were busy filling the shelves with replacements for the books they had sold during the last couple of weeks. The new books arrived in plastic storage boxes from their warehouse. Three or four of these boxes were stacked up on wheels and then dragged through a corridor by a porter to different departments of the shop. A member of staff called Ali was being paged on the shop's public address system. I discovered second-hand and remainders sections on one of the floors and was browsing in the second-hand section when the porter arrived with new stock for the remainders section in the adjacent room. He had seen me examining the spine of a book in a set of volumes that interested me. The porter told me that there were new copies in the plastic boxes he was dragging, going on sale as remainders. He opened one of the boxes and picked up a set of books to show me. It was an American import. The price of the new set was one-third that of the second-hand set. In the meantime, the PA system announced the name 'Ali' again. The porter excused himself as he had to go to the office on the top floor. I was glad that he had saved me money by arriving there on time with the new books. After this, I visited the shop every now and again.

Ali was always busy bringing in new stock of books or running errands for the different departments of the shop. I heard his name often called on the PA system. He was suitable for this kind of job because he was an obliging person. When I saw him again I thanked him for pointing me in the right direction the last time. He told me about the new acquisitions of the remainders section, which were going on sale in a few weeks time. Many good titles often ended up there. They were sold for less than half-price, whereas one paid two-thirds of the original price for second-hand books in this bookshop. Ali had been working as a porter for over ten years. Two or three of the assistants working in the bookshop had celebrated their silver jubilee some time ago. There were over two hundred employees working in the various departments. Most of them worked as selflessly as Ali to live up to the expectations of those who visited the shop from faraway places to find the books they wanted. Some booklovers came from other countries to buy books at this, their favourite bookshop. I overheard one such bibliophile saying to a shop assistant, 'The books I am buying are worth their weight in gold', while placing a heavy pile of them on the counter. There was also a coffee shop in the basement, which filled the whole shop with a rich aroma of ground coffee. It was in the coffee shop that authors read their works to an audience. On these occasions, it was Ali's job to find a dais and a microphone for the author, and additional chairs for the audience. It was difficult for the staff of one department to know those who worked for another department on a different floor. But all of them knew Ali by name, because in the evening he collected the books that had been picked up by the customers in one department and left in another.

After frequenting the shop for many months, I bumped into Ali in Brunswick Square. He was surprised to see me drifting from the bookshop in another direction. Ali told me that he lived in the area in one of the flats above Brunswick Shopping Centre. I was always disorientated to see this concrete precinct amidst the brickwork of Bloomsbury. It was certainly a far cry from the Brunswick Square of E. M. Forster and John Maynard Keynes. There were many cantilevered flats built above the shopping centre. I was not sure whether the balconies of these flats, enclosed in glass and iron, were used as conservatories or storerooms by the residents. Many of the flats belonged to the council, but some of them were privately owned. The big shopping centre listed businesses which had disappeared long ago. In fact, I saw only a few shops open for trading. The rest of them were empty, displaying the names of previous owners on their windows. Among the shops that were still trading in this desolate shopping complex was a big charity shop where a few elderly residents were browsing through old clothes. Out of curiosity, I walked into another shop under the cantilevered flats that was open for business. It was a second-hand bookshop. The bookseller was working on a computer behind a big untidy counter. I complied with a notice at the door, asking customers to leave their bags at the counter. An oriental-looking man who sat by the entrance was eating a hot meal in a takeaway box while speaking to the man behind the counter. It filled the shop with rancid fumes. There was also stale fruit lying on a table in the shop. I hurried towards the bookshelves to escape the smell. The first few bookcases displayed paperbacks arranged by the names of publishers rather than authors. The bookshop also stocked a big selection of videotapes. I tried to survey the shelves at the farther end of the shop, but the smell of hot food had reached there before me, mixing with the musty air. It sent me out of the shop quickly.

The shopping centre included a cinema that showed art-house films. I assumed that the films were meant for those who visited Bloomsbury during the day, not those who lived in the flats above the cinema. The council tenants came from diverse backgrounds. I saw a few elderly Bengali men carrying shopping bags from a supermarket in the shopping centre. None of the shoppers looked as if they would have enjoyed art-house films. I left the Brunswick Centre from its eastern side, away from the entrance of the cinema. The concrete structure looked less painful from this side.

I had attributed the name of Russell Square to the author of *A History of Western Philosophy*. Some years later I learned that in fact its name derived from the landlords who owned the ground. Russell Square Gardens looked lush, and there were pedestrians walking through the square. The benches along the pathways were occupied by solitary saunterers, and there was a café at one corner of the square, which served hot and cold drinks to those who liked to sit in the open-air.

Whenever Ali saw me on my subsequent visits to the university bookshop, he would stop for a chat. Ali came from Rabat in Morocco. Employees of the bookshop who were flying to Marrakesh for their holidays usually asked Ali for travel advice. But Ali told me that he himself had been to Marrakesh only once and he had only a vague idea of the town. However, he gave them general advice about travelling in Morocco. One day Ali was talking to me when a shop assistant called Joanna came to tell him that she had recently bumped into David, from another department, in Marrakesh. Sometimes, even customers said to Ali, 'Oh, we love Moroccan interiors and the food'. Moroccan restaurants had become fashionable in many neighbourhoods of London. Ali, who was a diffident person, was lost for words when he heard such remarks. One evening I heard a soft voice on the PA system announce that the bookshop was going to close in fifteen minutes. When I saw Ali again the following week, I asked him if it was him who made that announcement. He explained that as there was no one else in the office that evening he had had no choice. He was nervous about making a mistake in his speech and in any case disliked it that his own name was being made public every day on the PA system. I always heard an articulate voice making that announcement in the evening. The announcer had evidently perfected his art with years of practice. Those who worked in the shop remembered his exact words and seemed happy to hear them.

Ali didn't mind working as a porter in the bookshop. He had worked as a refuse collector for a year before joining the bookshop as a porter. He went around in a pick-up van to collect old furniture and other items from those who requested it from the council. Ali could not believe his eyes when he first saw what people got rid of from their homes. Some of the items were hardly used, and others could have been easily repaired. A few years later, Ali heard the story of a man who went around in his pickup van in wealthy London neighbourhoods to collect discarded items from the owners of big houses. He set up a business to sell those items to people living in less affluent neighbourhoods. It was believed that the removal man had bought a mansion for himself in Portugal. Ali himself had found many things for his home while working as a refuse collector.

I asked Ali what was it like to start a job at the university bookshop after working as a refuse collector. He said that for him it was like being transported from the nether world to the upper world. He felt liberated by casting off his uniform. He could come to work at the bookshop in whatever clothes he liked. It was a very civilized place to work in. It was quite by chance that Ali had seen a notice one day at the door of the university bookshop advertising a vacancy for a porter. It was a temporary position, but they decided to offer him a permanent job after a period of four months. He had proved to have the right disposition for the job. Having got used to being shouted at by his fellow workers in his previous job, Ali was surprised that people here spoke to him in whispers. He had also noticed that there was a change of attitude towards him among the residents of the Brunswick

Centre since he had started his new job. Whenever people in Bloomsbury asked Ali where he worked, he would declare with pleasure that he worked for the university bookshop. Ali liked the idea that employees could borrow books from the shop to take home. He liked to borrow books on history, and only had to pay two-thirds of the actual price if he decided to buy one of them. As an employee, he could also pick up a book from the shelf and read it in the coffee shop during his tea breaks. Unlike many businesses, the shop treated its employees as considerately as its customers.

I met Ali outside the bookshop one day during his lunch break. He was going to the students' canteen across the road to have something to eat and invited me to join him. One didn't have to be a university student to eat there. They didn't sell the food in the canteen at subsidized prices. The Filipino woman serving food in the canteen knew Ali as a regular diner and gave him a free drink with the food. Since I was with Ali, she very kindly also gave me a free drink.

There were a few students of the university working in the canteen kitchen, preparing food for their fellow-students. The Filipino woman gave advice to the students working in the kitchen on how to save money. She spoke so loudly to her kitchen staff that I could hear her whilst sitting in the canteen. A band of students were testing their musical equipment in an area at one end of the canteen; and a few Asian students surrounded billiard-tables in a glass-enclosed room adjoining the hall. The portions of food served in the canteen were generous. The chefs were considerate in taking the appetite of the students into account. I found the portion of food too big for me – the pasta-bake tasted good but it was very filling. Ali couldn't finish his portion either. I saw a group of students sitting at the next table who had finished all the food on their plates. One or two tutors came in to have lunch in the student's canteen. The female tutor among them, who walked with the support of a walking-stick, was very thin. She was served only a small portion of food. Perhaps she was also a regular diner like Ali. The food served in the canteen tasted good but the tea and coffee were awful. The students were evidently not bothered by this as they preferred effervescent drinks.

A banner went up on a fence near Russell Square every few weeks displaying a sign for a book fair in a hotel overlooking the Square. The hotel was built in terracotta, and at the end of each year its exterior was covered with gaudy Christmas decorations. The interior of the hotel was too ornate for my taste. It dissuaded me from visiting one of the monthly book fairs hosted by the hotel. Then one day, I left home determined to walk into that hotel. I chained my bicycle to a stand a short distance away. I used the main entrance: a big chandelier was hanging in the foyer, which led to a marble staircase. There I looked for a sign directing me to the ballroom where the book fair was taking place, and then walked down a hallway to reach it. The doors were manned by a gentleman wearing a suit and tie. Before I could go in, he asked me to deposit my bag at the counter of the cloakroom, which I noticed was named after Virginia Woolf. When I returned to the door without my bag, the doorman ushered me into the ballroom. Many people were already there. They had used a side entrance to come in.

I was enchanted by the names of the towns from which the booksellers had come: Berwick-upon-Tweed, Burton-upon-Trent, and Henley-on-Thames. The place-names were written under the names of the bookseller on old-fashioned signboards. The books were placed on thin folding shelves of ingenious design. I was fascinated to read the description of books: 'octavo', 'full brown gilt', 'calf with gilt borders', 'raised bands', 'decorative gilt panels', 'brown Morocco labels', 'gilt lettering', 'marbled edges' and 'endpapers'. I was travelling back to a time when inexpensive paperbacks were not yet produced. Then I looked up at the ceiling. It was fitted with several modern audiovisual devices, which ruined my illusion of being transported to an earlier era.

The booksellers at the fair had their noses in serious books, oblivious of the people who were circling their stalls. Sometimes, a bookseller would exchange greetings with another bookseller and they would inform each other about trade matters in an esoteric language. I had fallen among artisans whose private language I could not understand. The booksellers and their loyal customers belonged to the same older generation. I met my local librarian at the fair – he had bought a few books for himself – and he asked me what I was doing there. Perhaps I looked out of place to him among the old folks. I drifted into the next hall. The recesses in one wall were mirrored, creating an illusion of the book fair extending into yet another hall. A smaller room was used to serve tea and coffee to the buyers and sellers. There were many people carrying their purchases in bags which advertised the fair. For a long time I had failed to figure out what the letters, PBFA, stood for, on the verso and recto of a book used as a sign for the book fair. I discovered at the fair that it meant the Provincial Booksellers Fairs Association, which organized book fairs from Edinburgh to Dublin.

The book fair reminded me of an encounter I had had with a lady in another hotel a few weeks before. She had come there to attend an antiques auction. I met her after the auction had finished, about to go home with a big heap of antique furnishings. She told me that it was like an illness to be a collector of old things. She didn't have any more room at her home to use these furnishings, but her urge to buy them was stronger than the predicament of what to do with them. She was going to store the furnishings in her spare room. I asked her how she came to know about the auction. She said that it was advertised in a newspaper as a liquidation sale. I had seen those notices in newspapers many times, declaring the sale of 'confiscated goods by Her Majesty's Customs Department'. But I hadn't thought that people in London paid attention to mendacious notices in the newspapers: the goods were not confiscated by Customs but were bought from regular wholesalers. I asked the lady how much she had spent in the auction. She took the receipts out of her handbag and tried to do the sum on her fingers. She said that the auctioneers added VAT and other surcharges on top of the bid so she had spent more than she intended to: the total amount was approximately £5,000.

I left the book fair empty-handed, without buying a book. When I walked up Woburn Place, I saw a sign for another book fair in a hotel on the opposite side of the road. I turned into the courtyard of this hotel to see what differences might exist between two book fairs on opposite sides of the same street. When I enquired about this fair at the front desk of the hotel, the receptionist sent me across the courtyard to another wing of the hotel. It was more like a second-hand book sale than an antiquarian fair. The crowd was heterogeneous, and there were many people who were obviously hotel guests roaming about. It occurred to me that this hotel also hosted a fair for old comics two or three times a year, as I had met one of the dealers on a few occasions when he came to London from Atlanta to attend the fair. He usually stayed at the hotel I worked at. One day he left with me an A4-sized box full of comics to be shipped back to Atlanta. I asked him about the commercial value of the contents in order to fill out a declaration on the shipping form. To my astonishment, he said that it was $20,000. The comics in the box had been published before 1970. The prices of the books bound in calf-leather, their titles written in gilt lettering along the spines, which I had seen at the book fair across the road, suddenly looked cheaper to me than the old comics.

The university bookshop employees gathered once or twice a year in a pub near Goodge Street for a quiz night. There was fierce competition between various departments to win the first prize. It also arranged an end-of-the-year dinner for their staff in a restaurant in Central London. There were two banquets taking place in the restaurant that evening. I happened to be part of the other group. I recognized the employees of the university bookshop on the other side of the restaurant. They had dressed up for the occasion. I saw Ali, wearing a suit and tie, sitting in a corner with a very beautiful woman. I walked up to him for a chat and he introduced the woman sitting beside him as his wife. They had only recently married. Ali's wife, who was from Tunisia, was fluent in French but spoke little English. Many of the men who worked in the bookshop came to say hello to Ali's wife. They were so stunned by her beauty that they wanted to talk to her, even if her English was poor. The manager of the bookshop came to shake hands with the couple. Ali had transformed himself into Aladdin from *The Thousand and One Nights*, who strikes lucky one day by hearing the words 'Open Sesame', enabling him to enter a cave full of gold and silver. Ali had suddenly become a guest of honour. But being a shy person, he felt uneasy.

Although Ruskin had found it ugly, the architecture of

Gower Street fascinated me. The buildings were dated in roman numerals, which I could not decipher, and I had to guess when they were built. A redbrick building with conical towers was followed by symmetrical buildings made of blackened bricks. The statuettes on top of the entrance to the Royal Academy of Dramatic Art on the other side of the road captivated me. The corner of Keppel Street offered me a glimpse of the stern-looking Senate House in Malet Street. The intersection at the bottom of the road was busy with groups of pedestrians going to the British Museum. An Arab man was selling paintings of Egyptian gods and goddesses on the pavement outside the Museum. A man from Kosovo was selling hot dogs on the other side of the pavement. I walked past the Ionic columns towards the Round Reading Room of the British Library, in the labyrinths of which Borges, the blind Argentinean writer, was always fearful of losing himself. There were a few readers at the desks where Marx and Lenin had once sought refuge from a hostile world. The reading room was full of tourists and children. I left it to circumnavigate the Great Court, which was covered with a glass and steel roof fabricated in a chevron style. The roof amplified the voices of people in the Great Court. The washrooms around the Reading Room had mirrors fixed on opposite walls, creating reflections within reflections to perplex the onlooker.

I went back into the Reading Room to behold its dome. Diners sitting in an adjoining restaurant could see the readers through a glass window in the dome. The Reading Room was lined with concentric bookshelves, of which those at ground level were half empty. The books on these shelves were comparatively new. The volumes on the upper shelves looked antiquarian. The British Library had taken the Reading Room books with it to its new site. The shelves were filled again with a new collection that made the Reading Room more of a museum piece. Some of the shelves were filled with replica leather-bound books in place of the original volumes.

I entered a maze of desks in the Reading Room to find out what the new readers were absorbed in. Some of them were reading tabloid newspapers, others were busy reading their college textbooks. A few had picked up books from the shelves in the Reading Room. Serious researchers had also moved with the British Library to its new building. I returned to the entrance of the Reading Room after walking along a circular path. The azure, cream and gold dome was awe-inspiring. The Round Reading Room had been restored and the Great Court built around it with the help of Lottery funds. Gamblers had contributed money to a good cause.

I had known about the existence of the Round Reading Room only from books. When I visited the British Museum for the first time, the Reading Room was not open to the public, only to members of the British Library. I had caught a glimpse of a library room while entering the Museum. The room was now used for the sale of silks and ties. I had felt exhausted by touring the Egyptian galleries in the Museum on my first visit, paying very little attention to other exhibits. On my second visit, a vivacious lady, who was working as a voluntary guide, took me on a guided tour of the Mesopotamian capital of Ur. I came back two or three times to see the other collections in the Museum.

For some time I had confused the name *Elgin Marbles* with Antonio Canova's *The Three Graces* at the Victoria and Albert Museum. I had visited the Parthenon Gallery at the British Museum without realizing that its exhibits were known as the *Elgin Marbles*. Then I heard about the controversy surrounding them and wanted to visit the Parthenon Gallery again. I asked a security guard at the Museum for the room number of the Gallery. He pointed me towards the Great Court and instructed me to take a left from there. When I entered the Gallery, I saw the headless statues of Iris and Nereid in front of me. A curator was about to lecture a group of American youngsters on the *Elgin Marbles*, so I stayed to hear his account. The American teenagers already looked tired at the beginning of their tour of the Museum. The curator began by saying that the exhibits in the Gallery were known as the *Elgin Marbles* because the statues, which were made of marble, were removed by Lord Elgin from the Parthenon in Athens. Lord Elgin had offered baksheesh to the Ottoman Porte and got permission to remove any stones from the Parthenon, built 2,500 years ago to mark the final triumph of Greece over Persia following long and savage wars. It was commissioned by Pericles between 490–480 BC. The curator said that the statues were defaced when the temple was converted into a church, and there was a big explosion inside the temple when a Venetian missile had landed on a pile of gunpowder stored there by a Turkish garrison in the seventeenth century. The curator said that he wouldn't exaggerate the exposure of the temple to the elements when Lord Elgin removed marbles from it. Despite the incessant requests of the Greek government, neither Margaret Thatcher nor the current British Prime Minister wanted to return the Marbles to the land of their origins.

I walked to one end of the Gallery to witness the scene of the birth of Athena from the head of Zeus. The Greek goddess was surrounded by metopes depicting the struggle between Centaurs and Lapiths. The Centaurs, part man, part horse, were invited to the wedding feast but became drunk with wine and attempted to carry off the Lapith woman. It was unlikely that anyone would be moved by these Marbles without seeing pictures of the ruins of the temple from which they had been removed. On leaving the Gallery, Byron's words came to my mind:

'Dull is the eye that does not weep to see
Thy walls defaced, thy mouldering shrines removed...'

I had been to the Parthenon in Nashville, Tennessee – a replica of Athen's Parthenon, which, unlike the original, came complete with its *Elgin Marbles*. I had only vague memories of my visit to the replica Parthenon, built in a park, except that it was very humid in Nashville in August and I had felt nothing on seeing it.

When the curator asked the group to follow him to another room I decided to leave the Museum for a stroll. I drifted into Museum Street towards Bloomsbury Way and saw a house occupied by the Swedenborg Society. The aim of the society was to publish the works of Emanuel Swedenborg in English. The Swedish scientist had tried to show by scientific and logical analysis that the universe was of spiritual origin. I walked through Bloomsbury Square to get back to Great Russell Street. There were hordes of tourists climbing up the flight of steps to enter the British Museum. I turned into a side-street to walk around the Museum. There were a few big coaches parked at its north side. I found another entrance to the Museum used by very few people. I also discovered the other end of Malet Street. The university bookshop was located at the opposite end of the same street and I continued walking in that direction. It was a quiet road, with just a few vehicles driving along it. Soon after, I saw a cavalcade of vintage cars driving past at a gentle pace. The motorcade stopped ahead of me, and I caught a glimpse of Her Majesty the Queen alighting from one of the cars, to be ushered into the Vanburgh theatre. I felt no emotion whatsoever.

I hadn't seen Ali in the bookshop for many weeks. I asked someone who worked with him about his whereabouts. The porter said that Ali had given up his job there some time ago. But he didn't know what he was doing now. A year later, I saw Ali again walking near Tavistock Square. He had been unwell for a few months and he was going to see a doctor again that day. I asked Ali how long he had worked at the university bookshop. Ali said that he had worked there for twelve years and eventually tired of it. It was tiresome to work as a porter in a big bookshop. Ali said that he hadn't found any other work yet, but he wanted to recover his health before undertaking another job.

Across Waterloo Bridge

I usually watched the red buses crossing Waterloo Bridge from the Embankment. The bridge reminded me of a story by H. G. Wells I had read at school because it was here that a tramp offers diamonds for sale to the narrator. Sometimes I would walk over a footbridge for a panoramic view of Waterloo Bridge with the dome of St Paul's Cathedral in the background, on my way to South Bank. I filled the weekends at the Royal Festival Hall during my first year in London. I would venture out as far as the Hayward Gallery, and return from there on my trail home. When I heard the place-name 'Elephant and Castle' for the first time, it sounded fanciful to me. Then one day I boarded a bus to go there. As the bus drove down Waterloo Road, it felt as if I was travelling from one town into another. There were hardly any trees or greenery visible around there. The traffic on the road was very heavy. I was travelling along the Roman Road, built two thousand years ago to connect London with Dover.

When the bus reached Elephant and Castle, I saw a shopping centre built on a big roundabout, surrounded by a jumble of council estates. I got off the bus to meet an acquaintance in the shopping centre. The entrance looked like a market place. There were stalls selling bedlinen and soft furnishings. A footwear shop advertised itself as a factory outlet. The greengrocer sold cooking bananas and yams from Ghana. Another stallholder was selling African clothes. The place looked busy but I was not sure how people arrived here. I had difficulty crossing the road due to heavy traffic around the centre. I walked up an escalator to the first floor of the arcade. There was a big Western Union office on this floor. A luggage shop sold outsize suitcases. A South American man and a woman were busy on their sewing machines in an alterations shop built in the middle of the arcade. There were also a few generic fast food shops on the first floor.

I met my acquaintance in a coffee bar in the shopping centre. Isabel, who lived a short distance from the arcade in London Road, came from Venezuela and had been living in London for ten years, the last spent in penury. She had come to London as a student, then became the mistress of a Gujarati Khoja for the next eight years, until she was betrayed by him with another woman. Isabel had found life tough as an overseas student in London. She attended college during the day and worked as a waitress in an Italian restaurant in the evenings. It was there that she had met Asghar, who came every week to have dinner with his friends. Asghar, who liked to call himself Ash, was a flamboyant and generous person. At first Isabel had disliked him for being ostentatious but she liked his generosity. Asghar left hefty tips for her when he picked up the restaurant bills of his friends. It helped Isabel to pay her rent and college fees. Asghar would offer her a lift home in his car after she finished work, sometimes waiting until midnight for her.

Isabel knew that Asghar was a married man so she was unwilling to go out with him. But Asghar was persistent in his pursuit of her. He would go out of his way to do little things for her and she felt indebted to him. They saw each other often on various pretexts, and then Asghar started renting rooms in various four-star hotels in Central London on a day-let basis. I had seen Asghar many times in a hotel with different women. Everybody in the hotel knew that it cost him money even to sit down in the lounge with those women. He also brought his wife and children to the same hotel now and again. I was surprised to see Asghar in the Imam-bara at Stanmore one day, wearing black Kurta-pyjamas and solemnly observing Moharram.

Isabel had felt guilty in consorting with a man who already had a wife and children. But she discovered that Asghar had become emotionally dependant on her, like a child. Besides, he provided the support she needed to live in London as an overseas student and had even arranged the extension of her visa with the Home Office. Isabel had lived in a small flat, which she shared with three other students before she met Asghar. He rented a two-bedroom flat for her in West Hampstead. He also made her give up her job and become a lady of leisure. A few months later, Isabel gave up her studies.

For some time Asghar introduced Isabel as his secretary until he saw other men paying her attention, whereupon he introduced her as his girlfriend. He ran a wholesale business in electronic goods and owned a big house in Winchmore Hill and a warehouse in Edgware. He would leave his home in the morning to go to his warehouse, then went to see Isabel in the afternoon. I had seen them having lunch together many times in a café in West End Lane. They both looked radiant. As time went by, Isabel gradually came to know about Asghar's past. He had always kept mistresses; Isabel heard the sad stories of half a dozen women who had preceded her. Asghar had promised Isabel that he would marry her in due course, the same promise he had made to his other mistresses. But Isabel found it difficult to trust a man who cheated on his wife. In fact, she didn't mind him going back to his wife in the evening. It was his flirtations with other women which undermined her.

Asghar always sent Isabel on holidays on her own. He never accompanied Isabel on these trips abroad because of his business engagements. Nor did he accompany his wife and children on their holidays, for fear of antagonizing his mistress. Isabel was uncertain what Asghar was up to in her absence. She had caught him once or twice courting other women. She had a feeling that Asghar could be using the flat he had rented for her as a rendezvous when she was away from home. Asghar's wife, too, suspected there was another woman in her husband's life.

Isabel was getting older waiting for Asghar to fulfil his promise to her. One day someone told her that there was no obligation for Asghar to marry her because, like Wajid Ali Shah, the King of Oudh, he could have as many temporary wives as he could provide for. It was difficult for Isabel to live without Asghar's support, especially as she had become accustomed to a life of luxury. Her expenses were many times more than she could earn by taking a job. Isabel had found Gujarati Khojas to be both very astute businessmen and parsimonious. Asghar was the only generous person among them. Given their principles of parsimony, all the Gujarati Khojas were puzzled by Asghar's prosperity because he was always spending lavishly on them.

Isabel was surprised that Asghar was successful in his business of selling gizmos, about which he knew very little. He always took risks. Sometimes he made money on the new gadgets, at other times he lost. But business on the whole was profitable for him. He relied on others for such simple tasks as writing a cheque and paying an invoice. One day Isabel asked him his secret of success in business. He told her that his mother had prayed for him when she was alive. He also believed in luck playing a part. Asghar knew very well that there were far more intelligent men than him in London who had failed many times in business. He had very clever people working for him. One of them was a computer wizard who informed Asghar about new computer products on the market.

Asghar also attributed his success to the rise of Tottenham Court Road as the place to buy electronic goods in London. I became acquainted with this street a few months after my arrival in London when I wanted to buy a radio to keep my mind occupied in the evenings. The road was busy with audio and video equipment shoppers, many of whom looked as if they were only visiting London for a few days. Each shop was divided into counters run by different firms. The shopkeepers were mostly Asians. The prices of the same goods varied considerably from one shop to another. Expensive items were not priced: it seemed that the shopkeepers assessed a customer before quoting the price. They also confirmed the prices with each other on the phone. I wondered whether several of the stalls were owned by one person or all of them had a common supplier. The stallholders instantly recognized a shopper who went from shop to shop in search of a bargain. They communicated the price quoted to such a person to the next shopkeeper before that person had entered the next shop.

The Asian shopkeepers appeared prosperous to me, thanks no doubt to the incredible rise of the personal computer. It was Kasim's friend Gordon who had told me that, at the age of fifty, he went to buy a computer in Tottenham Court Road in order to find a job. He had to learn the new meaning of the word 'configuration' before hunting for a bargain at the south end of Tottenham Court Road. Gordon soon acquired computer skills that went beyond the scope of his search for a job. He found his newly acquired knowledge very useful in furthering his friendship with the shopkeepers around Charing Cross Road. He showed them how to find the various characters of their mother tongue by using the computer keyboard. I had heard about computers and their artificial intelligence when I was growing up in Kashmir. But I could never work out their usefulness in day-to-day life. It was like the bar code on the wrappers of foreign goods, which I considered to be a kind of cryptogram. After many years I was persuaded that one could indeed find a good bargain in the rapacious market place that was Tottenham Court Road. I had bought a second-hand computer which crashed after a few weeks, and took it to a big computer shop at the north end of Tottenham Court Road. The technician in the shop said that it would cost me an arm and leg if I wanted to have the computer repaired. I walked in despair to the busier end of the road and succeeded in finding a smaller shop. The shopkeeper called his technician down from a loft to assess the damage. He charged me very little money to repair the damage and I was delighted by the friendliness of the technician.

Asghar's strength in business came from his social skills. He had made many friends among the shopkeepers in Tottenham Court Road and he treated them to lavish dinners. They were themselves very tight-fisted. Many of them demanded commission from the taxi-drivers who picked up passengers from their shops. Some of them were richer than Asghar. But they were never as extravagant as he was. Asghar's generosity had helped him to win many friends. He supplied electronic goods to his friends, and offered better credit facilities to his clients than other suppliers. He also considered all of his customers as creditworthy. He trusted the people who worked for him, but he was mistrustful of his mistress; not in money matters but in the matter of her fidelity. Asghar often rowed with Isabel when he saw her with a male friend. Sometimes he arranged for his own friends to try her, in order to test her fidelity. However, these rows were like showers in the spring and didn't last long. After making her cry Asghar usually bought her flowers and chocolates. The row would start when they accused each other of infidelity, Asghar accusing Isabel to disguise his own dishonesty.

I asked Isabel how her relationship with Asghar had come to an end. She told me that Asghar had met another Venezuelan woman who, at twenty-five, was ten years younger than her and thirty years younger than him. Isabel had gone to Asghar's warehouse one afternoon, where she saw him frolicking with this other women, who looked abashed when Isabel entered the room. It occurred to Isabel that Asghar must have told her the same tale she had heard from him when they first met about how the other women in his life had mistreated him. Asghar had told the same story again and again to a number of women, all of whom found his sad tale very moving. It was only many years later that they realized how gullible they had been. Isabel was shocked that Asghar could leave her, just like that, for a younger woman, and suffered a nervous collapse after a few weeks of her break-up with him, from which she hadn't fully recovered. The radiance in her face was seemingly gone forever and she looked very sullen, despite having undergone therapy for the last year. She was evicted from her flat in West Hampstead and was obliged to move to cheap lodgings in Elephant and Castle. Isabel was unable to look for a job after her nervous breakdown. The doctors considered her unfit to work for a year. However, she was gradually coming to terms with the loss of her precious years and her beauty to a man who in the end had proved unworthy of her trust.

I was saddened to see Isabel in her adversity because in the past I would catch a glimpse of her looking very radiant while she sat in a nearby café. I left the shopping centre at Elephant and Castle after our meeting in a melancholy mood. The council estates close by the roundabout looked frightful. The tower blocks had dozens of satellite dishes fixed on their exterior walls – satellite television seemed to have a huge audience in this neighbourhood. The white curtains draping the windows of the flats in these blocks were blackened with dirt. A big banner on one of the buildings advertised accommodation to let on a short-term basis. The portico of the Metropolitan Tabernacle Church looked too grand in this setting. A pub near the shopping centre was named after Charlie Chaplin, reminding me of the great comedian's impoverished life while growing up in South London. From the shopping centre, I took a walk along New Kent Road. There were big council estates as far as the eye could see. When I reached the Old Kent Road, I saw many second-hand shops on both sides of the road. Many were like general stores. Some of the shops advertised 'Van & Man' for hire in big letters on their windows. Every other shop looked like a place for sending money abroad. Even the barbershop had a counter built inside for transferring money to different countries. There were also many Internet cafés along this road, and these shabby places were fully occupied.

Isabel had told me that the flats above the shops in Old Kent Road were rented by people from Bolivia, Columbia, Peru and Ecuador. They mostly worked as cleaners in Westminster and Whitehall offices. A few of them were lucky to find more lucrative work as window cleaners at shops in Mayfair and Knightsbridge. The office cleaners either worked late at night or in the early hours of the morning, and they often sent money to their families back home from the shops in Old Kent Road. After her nervous breakdown Isabel had found a kind of refuge among the South Americans living around Elephant and Castle. When she moved into their neighbourhood, they had given her support in her hour of need as she slowly recovered from her depression. After she had broken up with Asghar, it would have been difficult for

Isabel to fill her days living in West Hampstead. She had seen good times in West Hampstead, and it would have been difficult to go through her bad days living in the same neighbourhood without any means of support. She was known to the shopkeepers and café owners in the area as a lady of leisure who was accustomed to the fine things in life. She had bought orchids and calla lilies from a florist in West End Lane, who knew what flower colour and arrangements she preferred. The newsagent would put aside a copy of *¡Hola!* for her. Isabel had been generous in her dealings with shopkeepers and the waiting staff in cafés, so they usually went out of their way to get her the things she liked.

Isabel used to see an elderly lady walking with the help of a walking stick up and down West End Lane. The lady was very slender, and her body was bent forward at a right angle. She dressed elegantly, even though she went out only to buy a copy of the evening paper. Her hands were covered with white gloves. Someone had told Isabel that the elderly lady had been an opera singer many years ago, the mistress of a wealthy businessman for twenty years. The businessman had betrayed her when he died, leaving everything to his wife and children, nothing to the woman who had been loyal to him for twenty years. After this, she had managed on very little, but continued to wear elegant clothes and costume jewellery in her old age out of habit. When she lifted her head to a newsagent to pay for her daily paper, one could only guess how beautiful the ex-opera singer must have looked in her youth.

Watching the elderly lady on her walks, it had never occurred to Isabel that one day she herself would be betrayed by a man. Isabel had never thought of herself as a mistress. Asghar had succeeded in making her believe that he considered her to be his other wife. So she hadn't acted like a mistress by demanding expensive things. She had sent some money to her family in Caracas to help them to emigrate to California, but hadn't put any thing aside that would have seen her through her adversity. When Asghar left her, all she had was a few hundred pounds. She determined to leave that part of town.

When she moved to Elephant and Castle it was like going back to her old life of hardship. However, she made a few friends in the new neighbourhood, which made life bearable for her. Isabel had met a woman called Anna in the shopping centre at Elephant and Castle and they had become good friends. Anna worked as a cleaner in the homes of a few senile residents in the wealthy area of Belgravia. Among the homes Anna cleaned twice a week was that of a retired army officer. He had led a disciplined life and kept his home very tidy until he was eighty-five. His neighbours had told Anna that the retired officer had a deep disregard for working-class people, who lived, he believed, in disgusting conditions. Then his health took a downward turn and he became bedridden. Anna had found his home to be the only truly disgusting place she ever had to clean. She kept her own flat very tidy. Anna was a few years older than Isabel, and at thirty-eight had already become a grandmother. Six years ago, a year after her husband was killed in Bolivia, she had come to London in search of work. Her son had married in Bolivia two years ago and had fathered a child. Anna supported her son's family and two of her other children by cleaning homes in London.

Isabel had reconciled herself to the idea of living a sterile life. She had suffered a miscarriage and underwent an abortion when she was Asghar's mistress. It was unlikely that she would have children after having suffered a nervous breakdown. Anna introduced Isabel to her friends in South London. Many of them had small children and it gave Isabel pleasure to visit them at their homes. Sometimes, she would volunteer to babysit for them when they wanted to go out and she often got invited to the homes of her new friends in Elephant and Castle for dinner.

Isabel had been to West End Lane just once since leaving West Hampstead. She had walked furtively at dusk on one side of the road without taking a side-glance at the cafés and shops that she had frequented for many years. The shopkeepers would have been horrified to see her in such a sullen mood. She avoided the florist who had supplied the orchids and calla lilies for her living room. While crossing a railway bridge on West End Lane, Isabel thought about the day when she had left her flat in a demented state to throw herself under a train. She was glad that she had survived. A fleet of white limousines in a parking lot reminded her of the occasions when Asghar had hired stretch limos for her. She didn't know whether such gestures had meant anything to Asghar but they had meant a lot to her. Perhaps it had meant nothing unusual to Asghar, who was a spendthrift when it came to pleasing a woman. It occurred to Isabel now that he must have sent the same limousines to many women in his life. He would always conquer a woman with generosity. Isabel hadn't behaved like a mistress with Asghar, which she now deeply regretted. She had fallen in love with him, and it was her love for him that had undermined her in the end.

Asghar had been more considerate towards Isabel than other men who wanted to take her out when she was a student. He took pains in looking after her. Isabel had felt that she was intensely loved by a man for the first time in her life, so she didn't mind so much that he was already married. Besides, Ashgar's marriage was an arranged one. His wife came from another Khoja family in North London. Asghar had confided to Isabel that he felt unloved by his wife, who was in any case unattractive and left home only on rare occasions. Isabel had taken a chance in embarking on a relationship with Asghar, thinking that one day he might make an honest woman of her. She learnt a few years later that he had no intention of fulfilling her wish, and that was when their relationship began to falter and suspicions set in. Asghar was a possessive person. He didn't like Isabel to be friendly with any man but himself. He paid surprise visits to her flat. Isabel knew very well that he would find another mistress soon after saying adios to her, as there was no dearth of women in this town who would have liked to be in her shoes. However, she hadn't guessed that it could be someone from her own country. Asghar had got to know Venezuela and its customs through Isabel and thus it was easier for him to court another woman from the same country. When she was evicted from her flat in West End Lane, Isabel had felt very angry with Ashgar's new mistress. But now she had sympathy with that unfortunate woman.

I boarded a bus from Old Kent Road to Aldwych. In the midst of the shops on one side of Old Kent Road was a church called Mount Zion. It was a long way from the Metropolitan Tabernacle, opposite the shopping centre at Elephant and Castle, which had become famous for sermons given by a certain pastor. Solomon, the doorman, had told me that the Mount Zion in South London was frequented by many London-based Nigerians. The bus passed the big roundabout towards Waterloo Bridge. A group of children coming out of a school nearby had gathered near a bus stop. It looked as if no white pupils attended this school. When the bus reached The Cut, I saw a forlorn-looking Old Vic with a poster for *Hamlet* on its exterior. This was the first time I had embarked on a bus journey on the south side of the river in London. I had taken an overground train a few times from Waterloo to London Bridge, and the train had passed through a landscape that looked to me like an industrial wasteland. As the bus approached Waterloo Bridge, it offered me the prospect of a magnificent town on the other side of the river. I breathed the fresh air blowing over Waterloo Bridge. It was as if I had travelled through a nightmarish district. I suddenly realized that I had been to Lambeth and Southwark – the two boroughs in London that were notorious for their poverty.

The False Reputation
of Hampstead

I travelled by bus from Camden Town to Hampstead Heath.
The green and grey bus gained height before reaching the
fountain by South End Green. When I got off the bus and
walked towards the Heath, I caught the sight of woodland
and meadow for the first time in London. It was like a
homecoming for me after drifting through the various
neighbourhoods of London in search of work. It was a
Saturday afternoon in July and many people were arriving for
a picnic in the park. The first pond opened in my field of
vision like the landscape in Georges Seurat's *Sunbathers*. A
group of tramps was making merry by the next pond. One of
them was playing a guitar and another was dancing on
tottering feet. A woman in the group was feeding a dog from
the palm of her hand. The path inclined after the second
pond, and I could see many people on top of a hill trying to
locate landmark buildings in London.

The second time I visited this area, I travelled by tube
to Hampstead High Street. The train shed its load at Camden
Town, and the conversations of the passengers became

distinct and clear after the train had passed Chalk Farm. Two middle-aged women were talking about Sargent and Constable. I wondered why they were so fascinated by an army officer and a policeman. The tube station was located on a hill. There was a jovial guide waiting outside the station holding a placard for a walking tour of Hampstead village. I walked downwards towards the Heath. The High Street looked very nice with its boutiques and brasseries. The men sitting in the bars and cafés wore shorts and hats, but looked rather self-conscious in their casual gear. I stopped for a cup of coffee in one the cafés. The toilet sign was spelt as 'toilette' to make the café look more chic. Without a book or newspaper, I found the atmosphere in the café very oppressive. So I left soon after finishing my coffee. An artist displayed a few paintings on the pavement for sale while he worked on a fresh canvas. Close by, a homeless woman sold copies of a magazine to raise money for food. Two nannies were pushing strollers up the hill, engaged in conversation. I cut through Devonshire Hill to reach Hampstead Heath. In this road, a stockbroker was operating from a solitary shop with a baroque interior, in which computer screens on desks looked most incongruous. A wine bar was named after a nineteenth-century poet, its tables laid with brilliant white cloths. Where the road branched into two, someone asked me directions for Keats House, unaware that I was also new to the neighbourhood.

I found my first job in London in a corner shop in

South End Road. A year later, I rented a room in a house on South Hill Park. I spent two thirds of my meagre wages on the rent. I had heard about Hampstead for the first time in E. M. Forster's *A Passage to India*, in which an Englishman tells Dr Aziz that Hampstead is 'a thoughtful little suburb of London'. When I walked up South Hill Park to view a room to let in a house, I saw that many houses were for sale here. This was bewildering: if an Englishman's home is his castle, why do they sell them so often? After working in their neighbourhood for a year, I had succeeded in making how-do-you-do acquaintance with the people living in South Hill Park. If I had succeeded in engaging in small talk with the locals in the corner shop, I had also failed to be acknowledged by them outside the shop. I felt that the residents of South Hill Park looked at me a little awkwardly when they saw me walking up or down their road. I once got off my bicycle when I saw my next-door neighbour in Camden Town. She seemed overwhelmed by my gesture, yet I was only extending a common courtesy to her. I never stopped again on my bicycle for anyone walking on the pavement. On another occasion, I asked a lady who was trying to fix her bicycle in Tanza Road if she needed a hand. The lady didn't understand me. 'I beg your pardon?' she replied in astonishment.

My landlady was from Poland. She was looking after her mother in Warsaw and came to London every few weeks to collect the rent from her tenants. She kept the ground floor of the house for her own use and rented the rest of the house to four or five tenants. It took me a few months to see the other tenants living in the house. But I never saw the person who lived in the flat at the lower ground level. My room was on the top floor. I could see a part of the Heath from a window on the landing of each floor. It was the Heath which offered me consolation while living a solitary life in South Hill Park. There was a passageway leading to the Heath from there. I took a longer route through the Heath to the corner shop in the mornings. The weekends brought picnickers, but on weekdays I caught sight of other solitary people – an Italian woman with a poodle, a French woman with a spaniel who bought a copy of *Le Figaro* and a pack of Gauloises from me in the corner shop. The summer months were like a fiesta, with funfairs and open-air concerts. I spent my first few months in Hampstead in such diversions.

South Hill Park had a row of trees, which I could not name, on each side of the road. Sometimes a piano would break into a tune as I passed by a certain bay window on my way home. There were many creative people living in this neighbourhood. I felt as if God had made their hearts cold in return for creativity. I was trying to build friendships on the quicksand of the indifference of the people living in Hampstead. In my futile pursuit, I resembled a character in *À la recherche du temps perdu,* who searched in the realms of darkness for his lost Eurydice. I only realized some years later that Hampstead was an unlikely place to make friends. A woman, who had been running a shop in Hampstead for fifteen years, told me that she wouldn't want to live in Hampstead. She had found it difficult to meet the demands of a residents' association. Another shopkeeper told me that when he had started his business in Hampstead twenty years ago, the residents had opposed him tooth and nail. In the intervening years the same residents had experienced a change of heart and now found his business useful.

When winter set in, the Heath looked forlorn and barren. I took a walk as usual up to the Highgate ponds, which had been painted by melancholy artist, Howard Hodgkin, in vivid colours. These ponds looked desolate in winter light. Sometimes I would carry on walking until I reached a cemetery where George Eliot was buried. I had mistaken her name for a male writer, a misapprehension that was reinforced when I saw her picture. I pondered over my own isolation while passing by the catacombs in the cemetery.

I would take Highgate Road on my way back to the Heath. I had stayed in a hostel in this road during my second week in London. One day, I walked into this hostel again to use its cafeteria. It was empty. I sat in one corner with my nose in a book. A few minutes later, an American woman asked me if I minded her joining me. I didn't mind at all, but I was taken aback by her request. People in Hampstead find it excruciating to share a table with someone else in a café, preferring to wait for a table to become available. It would amount to incivility to ask a Hampsteadian to share a table with him or her in a café when other tables are unoccupied.

It would be enough to make them leave the place immediately. I had once made the mistake of asking a woman, whom I saw often in the corner shop, if I could join her at a table in a café in Hampstead. The woman seemed puzzled and looked pointedly at the empty tables. I realized my folly and rushed to a table at the far end of the café.

On my way home in the evenings, I usually noticed an Englishman entertaining two or three Japanese women in the dining room of his flat in a house in South Hill Park. The women seemed to be mesmerised by his conversations. My landlady told me that people in Hampstead liked to have Japanese women as tenants because they were very quiet and took off their shoes in the hallway before entering a room. She also said that these quiet Japanese women liked the High Street in Hampstead. I always avoided it while living in South Hill Park. If I ever had to go to the tube station in Hampstead High Street, I walked up Willow Road and turned into Flask Walk to reach it. One evening, I drifted into a labyrinth of alleyways near Flask Walk until I reached an estate which looked like old-fashioned blocks of council flats. A man was lying on the ground playing an acoustic guitar; another man was rolling up tobacco in cigarette paper. A woman was braiding the hair of a long-bearded man. In this neighbourhood of unsociable people, it looked like a veritable commune.

On one of her visits to London, my landlady brought two or three builders with her from Poland as she wanted to have her house renovated. She provided accommodation for the builders in her house, and gave them food. Perhaps she also gave them some pocket money for doing up her house. I moved out of South Hill Park without feeling any regret. I had lived like a pariah there for a year. I moved to the less fashionable lower end of the Heath, happy that I could still go for walks there. One morning, while going up East Heath Road, I saw a street-sign for 'Vale of Health', a charming name, I thought, for a road. I was curious about what kind of people lived in the seclusion of this vale. A few months later, I went to the Vale of Health on an errand and recognized a few faces among the residents. I saw them often in the corner shop buying newspapers and magazines. I had expected it to be a happy vibrant place. Instead, I was shocked to see the sullen faces of its residents.

The people who live in Hampstead have remained elusive to me during the ten years that I have lived in this area. It is the proximity of Hampstead to Central London that makes life bearable for me in this neighbourhood. I often travel by bus to the West End to spend my evenings. I have never entered The Freemason's Arms or Spaniards Inn in Hampstead to drown my sorrows. But I have attended a few lectures in Quaker House in hope of meeting a few English residents of Hampstead. Instead, I met Americans and Dutch. On Wednesdays and Sundays, I saw a group of Americans set out on a walking tour of Hampstead Village to see its cottages and mansions. They were guided by an

Englishwoman who had worked as an actress in various theatres. The Americans were captivated by her eloquence, especially when she baffled them now and again with a line from *Macbeth* or *King Lear*. The Americans came to Hampstead in search of local life in London. But the lady who guided them was the only person they could talk to in this neighbourhood. I once asked a guest at the hotel I worked in about Hampstead, where he had been for a day. He told me that it was picturesque, but as for the people: 'Oh man! They are chilly.' I could empathize with him. Among the artists whom I saw in the corner shop were one or two sculptors. Sometimes I felt that their hearts had turned as cold as the stones they worked on with their chisels.

My affliction in North-West London was also due to my own circumstances. In the words of Baudelaire, 'Of all those who have lost something they may not find / Ever, ever again!' I was in search of a hometown that had been lost. I understood that living in a sought-after neighbourhood in itself meant nothing. One could be living a tormented life while breathing the pure air on Mount Tyndall in Hampstead, and it was possible to live a joyous existence in the marshes of East London. One could also be beggarly even after owning a mansion in Hampstead. My life in Hampstead resembled that patch of the Heath that grows nettles in it for unknown reasons.

*

Although Camden Town was halfway between Hampstead and the West End, I bypassed it while cycling from Hampstead Heath to Central London. Someone in Hampstead once asked me if I had been to Camden Market. I knew it only as a few densely packed stalls outside the tube station, trading seven days a week. The person meant the weekend market, which attracted a big crowd. Then one weekend afternoon, I boarded a bus to go there. The landscape changed from suburban to phantasmagoric as the bus rolled down Haverstock Hill. Unicorns, artillery, and the bust of an Indian Chief appeared above the shop-canopies before the bus turned into Castlehaven Road. I got off the bus and entered a Victorian market hall. It was so crowded that I found it difficult to walk across it. A burly man wearing a red tailcoat and a wig stood at the entrance of the Stables Market. He rang a bell to attract the people inside. I was overwhelmed by the festivity as I entered this fortified market place. Oriental women selling food were shouting like street hawkers. There were shops inside the railway arches selling vintage clothes. The sound of African drums pulled me into the catacombs, becoming louder as I approached its entrance. There was a sweet smell of burning marijuana, and the atmosphere was ritualistic. Beyond that outpost, there were spacious shops selling furniture, kelims and sarongs. One of the shops displayed original railway furniture. An Englishman had posted a notice at his shop entrance saying 'No Taking Photos' as a gesture of goodwill to visitors. A dandy market trader was casting a spell on a group of women with his spiel. In an adjacent shop, the shopkeeper was wearing a kaftan to make it look like a souk. A white-bearded man sold old carpentry tools in the forecourt of the shop in the spirit of a Shaker. The shop across the yard displayed Javanese wooden masks and mirrors in their hundreds. A nearby workshop stocked restored furniture in oak. As I was leaving the Stables, I began to admire the commercial foresight of someone who had turned a horse hospital, a gin house and a wasteland into a teeming market place.

I once made the mistake of asking a picture framer in Hampstead if he had any less expensive frames in his shop. He scornfully replied that I should go to Camden Town if I wanted a cheaper framer. I realized that this was the wrong question to ask in such a snobbish neighbourhood. Unlike the boutiques of Hampstead, Camden Town has many useful shops, such as a hardware merchant, a haberdasher and bicycle shops. But I was fearful of going to Camden Town in the beginning. There were pawnbrokers and betting shops along its main road. When I passed Mornington Crescent on the way to Camden Town for the first time, I saw a pawnbroker's sign on a derelict building: 'Money advanced on pictures, bronzes and violins'. I was disturbed to see so many men and women wasted by drugs and drink. I could not understand why so many of them were standing outside the tube station. Most of them spoke in monologues. Some were carrying their bedding under their arms. The tramps of

Hampstead looked dignified to me in comparison. On my way to Hampstead I passed a bathhouse. One of its entrances had 'Men's First Class' inscribed on it, and the other had 'Men's Second Class'. I wondered how, in the days when those baths were built, they could divide unwashed men into two classes.

A towpath from the Lock led to a yard, in which one or two canal boats were moored that were used for trips from Camden Lock to Little Venice. This place-name, invented by Robert Browning, had evoked Canaletto's Venice in my mind. I was curious for many months to see Little Venice. Then I travelled there by a coffin-like canal boat. It was a disused canal, filled with stagnant water. Signposted to Birmingham and Liverpool, the canal followed a desolate route between warehouses and other grim-looking buildings. Now and again, a few homeless people appeared, walking along the footpath on one side of the canal. The boat reached a bulge in the canal where narrow boats were moored to the bank. This was Little Venice. I felt misled by Robert Browning's allusion and determined never to visit this neighbourhood again.

Camden Market attracts many students and people who believe in New Age mysticism. Many shops sell incense. In one of the Camden Market precincts, I met one or two stallholders who lived in Hampstead and greeted me. I was touched by their civility. The market brochure boasted that it promoted artists and young designers. But one of the stallholders told me that he was struggling, like many other stallholders, to pay his weekly rent to a big landlord. There was a large turnover of stallholders in the market. People, who came from faraway places to shop at Stables Market to support small businesses little realized that it was the landlord who benefited from their purchases. The stallholder said that he had fallen two weeks behind in paying his rent and was expecting a visit from one of the security guards employed by the landlord. He felt threatened by the presence of so many security guards in the market. The landlord had recently built many more new stalls, thus increasing the competition in the market. Many stallholders were selling the same merchandise. The stallholder pointed out the owner of the market among a group of builders. He looked very rough in his builder's gear. The stallholder told me that the market was worth a large sum and that the landlord had increased its value considerably in the last few years. I said goodbye to the stallholder and made my way to a tea-stall. The woman who ran it asked me if I was a market trader, so that she could give me a discounted price. I was touched by her generosity.

I went to Kenwood House for the first time with Cass, an American woman who lived in Hampstead. She was from Mill Valley in Marin County, and she was my only social contact in Hampstead for many months. I had been invited by many people to their homes in Mill Valley during my few months in Marin County. But I had failed in London for many years to enter a single English home. Sometimes I would find the lady who guided people on a walking tour of Hampstead explaining to her group the symbolic meaning of the wrought iron pineapples on the fences of the houses in Hampstead Village, which according to her meant 'welcome'. Whenever I heard her telling gullible visitors this, it made me smile.

I had met Cass in a café in South End Road. When she told me that she came from Marin County, it brought back happy memories of Mill Valley. She asked me if I had been to Kenwood House on the other side of the Heath and invited me to join her on a walk there. Cass, who was married to an Englishman, had moved to Parliament Hill a year ago. She was shocked by the reticence of people in her new neighbourhood. But she could not understand why people who were so given to understatement described everything as 'brilliant'.

I was glad to discover Kenwood House and its environs at the north side of the Heath. There were many people in the Brew House having tea and scones. I liked the trellis arbour, which led to a flower garden. The sham bridge over a pond near the concert amphitheatre looked real to me from a distance. There were a few elderly couples sitting on the benches along a gravel path. We left Kenwood House towards Hampstead Lane. There were big mansions on the other side of the road. One of the roads was marked as private and was blocked by a barrier, which was controlled by a watchman sitting in a cabin. It was the wealthier side of

Hampstead, designed by Edwin Lutyens. We passed Whitestone pond on top of this road towards Heath Street.

I visited the Tate Britain a few years after my arrival in Hampstead. When I saw the dreadful landscapes painted by John Constable, it reminded me of the middle-class women in Hampstead who raved about these paintings. I could not accept Forster's description of Hampstead as 'a thoughtful little suburb of London'. It had been painful for me to live in this neighbourhood. Its landscape, like the paintings of Constable, was very gloomy. It was an area where people apologized often but showed little kindness to others.

I became familiar with Camden Town after bypassing it for many years. I found that the people in Camden who wore combat clothes, and of whom I had been fearful, were in fact peace-loving folks. I preferred to sit in a crowded coffee shop in Camden Town rather than to go to a café in my own neighbourhood. The people working in the coffee shops in Camden were friendlier than those who served in the cafés in Hampstead. The students who worked in the crowded coffee shop in Camden were mostly Spanish and Italians.

On an autumn's evening, I saw Hampstead Heath illuminated by a full moon. It was a bizarre sight for me after living at one end of the Heath for several years. Just like freak weather, it attracted a few residents to gather on top of Parliament Hill. It had taken me a long time to reconcile to the idea of calling a 30-metre elevation a hill. I walked up the hill to see the town painted silver by the light of the moon. On a clear night, the city lights looked bright. These lights were dimmed on this occasion by the moon on the horizon. It reminded me of my moonlight strolls in Srinagar and the years that had elapsed since I left the valley of Kashmir. Standing on top of Parliament Hill created a false impression in an onlooker that the town was laid out just across a field and that St Paul's Cathedral was a short walk away. It was rather like walking across mountain valleys, when a trekker feels a mountain peak moving away from him, the further he walks towards it.

The next day I walked up Hampstead High Street, which I had avoided for many years. I noticed that the people I had seen there before had grown older. Halfway along the High Street, I saw an elderly man struggling to reach a slot in the post-box. When I reached him, I recognized his face. I remembered him as being a very genial person whom I knew as a customer when I worked in a corner shop in Hampstead. I was moved by his kindness whenever he came into the shop. It brought tears to my eyes to see him become senile. He used to wear a different suit and polished shoes every day. I saw that this time his shoes were grubby. It made me conscious of the years I had spent in the neighbourhood. I felt melancholy to realize how many years had been lost. It occurred to me that perhaps I shouldn't have made my natural shyness a virtue, and made a greater effort to assimilate.

September 2003 – May 2004

Acknowledgements:

My sincere gratitude to many

independent booksellers for

their invaluable support.

ALSO BY IQBAL AHMED

Empire of the Mind

A journey through Great Britain

As a young boy in Kashmir, Iqbal Ahmed imagined England as the mother country of the Empire, full of wonders. As an adult, he goes in search of the nation he once dreamt of, visiting the cities and towns of his imagination. On the way he encounters immigrants who struggle with unfamiliar culture and the issue of belonging. Iqbal's journey reveals a harsher but no less fascinating picture of modern British society.

Praise for *Empire of the Mind*

'A great tenderness of spirit suffuses this book.'

Independent on Sunday

'The literary equivalent of stopping in your tracks for a moment and looking about you. Sometimes, though, we don't have time. We need writers to do this for us. Iqbal Ahmed is one such writer.'

Lillian Pizzichini

'Fascinating, humorous and poignant.'   *The Times*

'Brilliantly observes the chilly, rootless life lived by many immigrants.'   *Independent*

Available in all good bookshops for £7.99